The Rational Guide To

SQL Server 2005
Express
Beta Preview

PUBLISHED BY

Rational Press - An imprint of the Mann Publishing Group
710 Main Street, 6th Floor
PO Box 580
Rollinsford, NH 03869, USA
www.rationalpress.com
www.mannpublishing.com
+1 (603) 601-0325

ISBN: 1-932577-16-5
Library of Congress Control Number (LCCN): 2005928284
Printed and bound in the United States of America.
10 9 8 7 6 5 4 3 2

Trademarks

Mann Publishing, Mann Publishing Group, Agility Press, Rational Press, Inc.Press, NetImpress, Farmhouse Press, BookMann Press, The Rational Guide To, Rational Guides, ExecuGuide, AdminExpert, From the Source, the Mann Publishing Group logo, the Agility Press logo, the Rational Press logo, the Inc.Press logo, Timely Business Books, Rational Guides for a Fast-Paced World, and Custom Corporate Publications are all trademarks or registered trademarks of Mann Publishing Incorporated.

All brand names, product names, and technologies presented in this book are trademarks or registered trademarks of their respective holders.

Disclaimer of Warranty

While the publisher and author(s) have taken care to ensure accuracy of the contents of this book, they make no representation or warranties with respect to the accuracy or completeness of the contents of this book and specifically disclaim any implied warranties or merchantability or fitness for a specific purpose. The advice, strategies, or steps contained herein may not be suitable for your situation. You should consult with a professional where appropriate before utilizing the advice, strategies, or steps contained herein. Neither the publisher nor author(s) shall be liable for any loss of profit or any other commercial damages, including but not limited to special, incidental, consequential, or other damages.

Credits

Author:	Anthony T. Mann
Technical Editor:	Roger Wolter
Copy Editor:	Jeff Edman
Book Layout:	Molly Barnaby
Series Concept:	Anthony T. Mann
Cover Concept:	Marcelo Paiva

All Mann Publishing Group books may be purchased at bulk discounts.

The Rational Guide To

SQL Server 2005
Express
Beta Preview

Anthony T. Mann

**RATIONAL
PRESS**

An imprint of the
www.mannpublishing.com

About the Author

Anthony T. Mann is the President/CEO of the Mann Publishing Group, which specializes in publishing business and technology titles, including this book (under the Rational Press imprint). He typically focuses on writing and teaching Microsoft-based technologies, including SQL Server, software development, and Microsoft Office. His 13 prior books include:

- ▶ The Attorney's Guide to the Microsoft® Office System (Agility Press)
- ▶ The Paralegal's Guide to the Microsoft® Office System (Agility Press)
- ▶ The Rational Guide To Microsoft® Virtual PC 2004 (Rational Press)
- ▶ The Rational Guide To SQL Server Reporting Services (Rational Press)
- ▶ .NET Web Services for Dummies (John Wiley & Sons)
- ▶ Microsoft SQL Server 2000 for Dummies (John Wiley & Sons)
- ▶ SharePoint Portal Server: A Beginner's Guide (Osborne/McGraw-Hill)
- ▶ Microsoft SQL Server 7 for Dummies (John Wiley & Sons).

He can be reached for comment or feedback about this book at tmann@mannpublishing.com.

Acknowledgements

I would like to express my sincere appreciation to all the people who have painstakingly produced this book, especially Jeff Edman. Jeff has managed in this project to keep me in line as deadlines loomed in the near distance. Since Murphy's law of software always dictates that beta versions don't work when you have deadlines, that made Jeff's job more difficult.

I also want to thank Roger Wolter, who tech edited this book. Roger is the Group Program Manager at Microsoft for SQL Server Express. He helped to ensure that the information contained in this book is as up-to-date and as accurate as possible. He was very responsive and a real pleasure to work with.

Once again, I would like to thank the love of my life — my wife of ten years, Alison.

About Rational Guides

Rational Guides, from Rational Press, provide a no-nonsense approach to publishing based on both a practicality and price that make them rational. Rational Guides are compact books of fewer than 224 pages. Each Rational Guide is constructed with the highest quality writing and production materials — at an affordable price. All Rational Guides are intended to be as complete as possible within the 224-page size constraint. Furthermore, all Rational Guides come with bonus materials, such as additional chapters, applications, code, utilities, or other resources. To download these materials, just register your book at www.rationalpress.com. See the instruction page at the end of this book to find out how to register your book.

Who Should Read This Book

This book is for anyone who wants to get an early look at using SQL Server 2005 Express. This can include professional software developers, architects, hobbyists, and non-professional developers. This book was written using the April Community Technology Preview (CTP) version of SQL Server 2005 Express and the Beta 2 version of Visual Studio 2005. While every attempt was made to ensure 100% accuracy in this book, it is, after all, based on beta software. As Microsoft releases future CTP and Beta versions, the functionality may differ slightly from that which is contained in this book. However, it will be close enough for you to get started with SQL Server 2005 Express.

Conventions Used In This Book

The following conventions are used throughout this book:

▶ *Italics* — First introduction of a term.

▶ **Bold** — Exact name of an item or object that appears on the computer screen, such as menus, buttons, dropdown lists, or links.

▶ `Mono-spaced text` — Used to show a Web URL address, computer language code, or expressions as you must exactly type them.

▶ **Menu1**⇨**Menu2** — Hierarchical Windows menus in the order you must select them.

Tech Tip:
This box gives you additional technical advice about the option, procedure, or step being explained in the chapter.

Note:
This box gives you additional information to keep in mind as you read.

Bonus:
This box lists additional free materials or content available on the Web after you register your book at `www.rationalpress.com`.

Caution
This box alerts you to special considerations or additional advice.

Contents

Contents

Contents

Contents

Overview

Chapter 1

Introducing SQL Server 2005 Express

The Express edition of SQL Server 2005 is completely free! How's that for a powerful first sentence in a book? It is a scaled-down edition of Microsoft's flagship database product, SQL Server. SQL Server 2005 is the latest version, which provides lots of improvements over its predecessor, SQL Server 2000. Probably the most notable enhancement is the integration of Microsoft's .NET technology into the SQL Server platform.

SQL Server 2005 Express can be considered an upgrade for the Microsoft Desktop Engine (MSDE), which as a scaled-down edition of SQL Server 2000. It provides many of the same improvements to MSDE as SQL Server 2005 does for SQL Server 2000. This chapter explores the enhancements that SQL Server 2005 Express provides over MSDE, along with a comparison of the features that are in all editions of SQL Server 2005, so you'll have a handle on when to upgrade to "non-free" editions of SQL Server 2005. Furthermore, this chapter outlines possible scenarios for using SQL Server 2005 Express. To begin, this chapter dives into some terminology that will be helpful for you to use while reading the rest of this book.

SQL Server 2005 Terminology

There are a few terms and concepts that are important for you to know before diving into this book. These terms are used throughout this book, so the earlier you grasp the concepts, the better. Each is described in the next few sections.

Instances

A SQL Server 2005 Express *instance* is a term that refers to a running incarnation of the database engine. You can think of an instance as a way to run multiple SQL Servers on a single computer. There are two types of instances in SQL Server 2005 Express:

▶ **Named Instance** — An instance that is always referred to by name. This name is specified during the installation process. It is recommended that SQL Server 2005 Express be installed on a named instance, called **SQLExpress**. This name is used to clearly differentiate a running instance of the Express edition of SQL Server 2005 over another instance of a different edition that might be running on the same computer. While this is not a requirement, it is strongly recommended that you stick with the named instance of **SQLExpress**.

▶ **Default Instance** — Main instance that does not need to be referred to by name.

Schemas

In SQL Server 2000, an object, such as a table, belonged to an owner, which corresponded to either a login name or was flagged as being owned by a database owner. If the object belonged to the database owner, it was flagged as **dbo**. With SQL Server 2005, a slightly different concept is implemented, known as a schema. A *schema* is a container for objects in a database. A schema, noted by a *schema name*, allows multiple tables with the same name to exist in a database. For example, if you have a schema name called **operations** and another one called **history**, you can have the same table named **customers** residing under each schema name.

You do not technically have to specify a schema name when you create objects in SQL Server 2005. However, if you don't, SQL Server itself will assign the object to a default schema named **dbo**. The **dbo** schema makes it backwardly compatible with SQL Server 2000.

Tech Tip:

When a database is upgraded to SQL Server 2005 Express, a new schema is created and has the same name for every user in the database. For example, a user named **Jeff** will have a new schema created called **Jeff**, which is owned by **Jeff**.

SQL Server 2005 Express Enhancements

As you learned at the beginning of this chapter, SQL Server 2005 Express is the upgraded replacement technology for MSDE, which is based on SQL Server 2000. It includes many requested enhancements over what MSDE provided. These enhancements are shown in Table 1.1.

Feature	SQL Server 2005 Express	MSDE
Active Directory registration	Yes	Yes
CLR /.NET Integration	Yes	No
Graphical Tools	Express Manager	No
Max CPUs	1	2
Max DB Size	4GB	2GB
Max RAM	1GB	2GB
Merge Replication	Yes, but only as a subscriber	Yes
Service Broker	Yes, but limited	No
Snapshot Replication	Yes, but only as a subscriber	Yes
SQL Agent	No	Yes
Transactional Replication	Yes, but only as a subscriber	No
Visual Studio Integration	Yes	No
Workload Governor	No	Yes
Xcopy Deployment	Yes	No

Table 1.1: SQL Server 2005 Enhancements Over MSDE.

The most notable enhancements in SQL Server 2005 Express over MSDE are available simply because of the upgrades in functionality between SQL Server 2000 and SQL Server 2005. Most of these are outlined in the next section, "SQL Server 2005 Editions." Other notable enhancements over MSDE are the removal of a workload governor, the inclusion of a graphical administration tool called Express Manager, and the bigger maximum database size. However, the maximum amount of memory has been reduced, as has the maximum number of CPUs. The SQL Agent has also been removed, so you cannot schedule automatic tasks with SQL Server 2005 Express.

SQL Server 2005 Editions

To understand the major features that are available in each edition, see Table 1.2. Pay particular attention to the features that are in the Express edition of SQL Server 2005. Note that the core database features that are important for any mainstream database are available in the Express edition. It is mainly the advanced features that are not available in SQL Server 2005 Express, which makes it perfectly suited for many different types of applications. For a detailed look at these scenarios, see the section "SQL Server 2005 Express Scenarios" later in this chapter.

CORE ENGINE				
Enhancement	Edition			
	Enterprise	Standard	Workgroup	Express
64-bit support	Yes	Yes	Yes, but runs in 32-bit	Yes, but runs in 32-bit
Automatic Tuning	Yes	Yes	Yes	Yes
Database Tuning Advisor	Yes	Yes	Yes	No
Express Manager	No	No	No	Yes
Full Text Search	Yes	Yes	Yes	No
Management Studio	Yes	Yes	Yes	No
Max CPUs	No limit	4	2	1
Max DB size	No limit	No limit	No limit	4GB
Max RAM	No limit	No limit	3GB	1GB
Parallel Indexing	Yes	No	No	No
Partitioning	Yes	No	No	No
Serviceability Enhancements	Yes	Yes	Yes	Yes
SQL Agent Job Scheduling Service	Yes	Yes	Yes	No

Table 1.2: SQL Server 2005 Editions.

PROGRAMMABILITY				
Enhancement	**Edition**			
	Enterprise	Standard	Workgroup	Express
Common Language Runtime and .NET Integration	Yes	Yes	Yes	Yes
Native XML	Yes	Yes	Yes	Yes
Notification Services	Yes	Yes	No	No
Service Broker	Yes	Yes	Yes, but must have Enterprise or Standard Edition in message chain	Yes, but must have Enterprise or Standard Edition in message chain
Stored Procedures, Triggers, and Views	Yes	Yes	Yes	Yes
T-SQL Enhancements	Yes	Yes	Yes	Yes
User-defined Types	Yes	Yes	Yes	Yes
XQuery Support	Yes	Yes	Yes	Yes
SECURITY				
Enhancement	**Edition**			
	Enterprise	Standard	Workgroup	Express
Advanced Auditing, Authentication, and Authorization	Yes	Yes	Yes	Yes
Best Practices Analyzer	Yes	Yes	Yes	Yes
Data Encryption and Key Management	Yes	Yes	Yes	Yes
Integration with Microsoft Baseline Security Analyzer	Yes	Yes	Yes	Yes
Integration with Microsoft Update	Yes	Yes	Yes	Yes

Table 1.2: SQL Server 2005 Editions (continued).

INTEGRATION				
Enhancement	**Edition**			
	Enterprise	Standard	Workgroup	Express
Import/Export	Yes	Yes	Yes	Yes
Integration Services	Yes	Yes, but only basic transforms	No	No
Merge Replication	Yes	Yes	Yes, but only 25 subscribers	Yes, but subscriber only
Oracle Replication	Yes	No	No	No
Transactional Replication	Yes	Yes	Yes, but only 5 subscribers	Yes, but subscriber only
Web Services (HTTP Endpoints)	Yes	Yes	No	No
ADVANCED FEATURES				
Enhancement	**Edition**			
	Enterprise	Standard	Workgroup	Express
Advanced data management	Yes	No	No	No
Advanced Performance Tuning	Yes	No	No	No
Analysis Services	Yes	Yes	No	No
Backup Log-shipping	Yes	Yes	Yes	No
BI Development Studio	Yes	Yes	No	No
Business Analytics	Yes	Yes, but not advanced	No	No
Data Mining	Yes	Yes	No	No

Table 1.2: SQL Server 2005 Editions (continued).

ADVANCED FEATURES (continued)				
Enhancement	Edition			
	Enterprise	Standard	Workgroup	Express
Data Warehousing	Yes	Yes	No	No
Database Mirroring	Yes	Yes, but full safety and single threaded	No	No
Enterprise Management Tools	Yes	Yes	No	No
Failover Clustering	Yes	Yes, up to 2 nodes	No	No
Fast Redo	Yes	No	No	No
Full writeback support	Yes	No	No	No
Online Indexing	Yes	No	No	No
Online Page and File Restore	Yes	No	No	No
Online System Changes	Yes	Yes	Yes	Yes
Proactive Caching	Yes	No	No	No
Service-Oriented Architectures	Yes	Yes	No	No
Text Mining	Yes	No	No	No
Unified Dimensional Model	Yes	Yes	No	No
Web Services support	Yes	Yes	No	No

Table 1.2: SQL Server 2005 Editions (continued).

SQL Server 2005 Express Scenarios

There are an unlimited number of scenarios where SQL Server 2005 Express can be deployed. Because the maximum database size has been increased over its MSDE counterpart, it is useful in more situations. Here are some possible scenarios to give you food for thought on how you can use SQL Server 2005 Express:

▶ Manufacturing scenarios where small databases are used at each station and are periodically replicated to a central database server. This scenario stores a small amount of information in many different workstations, such as the scanning of parts, picking of stock from bin locations, and more. However, all of this data needs to be aggregated and stored in a central repository for analysis.

▶ Retail scenarios where Point of Sale (POS) registers store transaction information and either send Service Broker messages to a central database server, or are replicated to a central database server. Much like the manufacturing scenario, the POS data is not very sizable, but also needs to be aggregated into a central repository.

▶ ISVs that develop applications that need database support. This is a very common scenario, in which a small database might store catalog information, configuration data, user profiles, and more. The database is administered and managed through an Independent Software Vendor's application.

▶ Students learning how to design, develop, and deploy SQL Server-based applications. Because this edition is free, it is perfect for the classroom. Students can even have a version on their personal computers or laptops, as well as classroom computers.

▶ Hobbyists who "play around" with databases and build data-driven applications, either Web-based, .NET class libraries, or WIN32-based applications.

Summary

Many improvements have been made in SQL Server 2005 Express over its MSDE predecessor simply because of the dramatic enhancements made to all editions of SQL Server 2005, such as the inclusion of CLR / .NET integration into the database engine. However, there are some key concepts in this free edition of SQL Server that have been enhanced over MSDE also. With the maximum database size effectively being doubled, there are more scenarios under which SQL Server 2005 Express can be effectively deployed.

Chapter 2

Installation

Installation of SQL Server 2005 Express is quite simple. Once you acquire SQL Server 2005 Express, you use a wizard to perform your installation. You can configure advanced options, but usually the default options available during the installation process will be sufficient for most users. This chapter outlines how to acquire, install, and patch SQL Server 2005 Express.

Acquiring SQL Server 2005 Express

Acquiring SQL Server 2005 Express is very easy. Because this is a free edition of SQL Server 2005, it is expected to be available in any of the following venues:

▶ **Microsoft SQL Server Web Site** — Visit the SQL Server Web site at `www.microsoft.com/sql/downloads/` for more information.

▶ **Microsoft Developer Network (MSDN) downloads** — Browse to `msdn.microsoft.com/downloads/` and search for SQL Server 2005 Express.

▶ **Independent Software Vendors (ISVs)** — Software vendors will be distributing SQL Server 2005 Express with their applications, just as they do for MSDE applications.

▶ **Microsoft Conferences** — CD-ROMs will likely be available at developer-related conferences, such as Microsoft TechEd and the Professional Developer's Conference (PDC).

Performing the Installation

If you have any beta or Community Technology Preview (CTP) version of SQL Server 2005 Express, you must first uninstall it, along with any beta version of Visual Studio 2005 and any beta version of the .NET Framework 2.0. Microsoft carefully coordinates the builds of all of these products together, so they may not work correctly if you don't uninstall all beta versions of these products from older builds. The April CTP version of SQL Server 2005 Express was used to write this book, so later builds may appear slightly different, but the concept is the same. To learn how to uninstall SQL Server 2005 Express, see the section "Uninstalling SQL Server 2005 Express" later in this chapter.

For CTP versions of SQL Server 2005 Express, you have to install programs separately:

▶ **.NET Framework 2.0** — Provides core services needed by SQL Sever 2005 Express and Visual Studio 2005 Express. The version of the .NET Framework 2.0 must match the SQL Server 2005 Express version and the Visual Studio 2005 Express version. If you are not sure if you have the correct version of any of these pieces, you can visit the SQL Express Web site at www.microsoft.com/sql/express.

▶ **SQL Server 2005 Express** — Database engine.

▶ **Express Manager** — Graphical tool for managing SQL Server 2005 Express

▶ **Documentation and Samples** — Books Online and sample databases.

▶ **Visual Studio 2005 Express** — Development tool for writing SQL Server 2005 Express applications.

Assuming that you have acquired the .NET Framework 2.0, SQL Server 2005 Express, Express Manager, and Documentation and Samples, you simply run the installation programs. However, SQL Server 2005 Express has some setup options, so its setup is covered in this chapter. The other setup programs are simple enough that their installation is not covered in this chapter.

To set up SQL Server 2005 Express, follow these steps:

1. Launch the setup program after you acquire it. This setup program is used to not only install a SQL Server instance for the first time, but also additional instances after the first one is installed. Starting with the June CTP, there are two versions of the setup program. **sqlexpr.exe** can be installed on 32-bit or 64-bit machines, while **sqlexpr32.exe** is used only on 32-bit machines.

Tech Tip:

It is strongly advised that your first instance be called SQLExpress to clearly differentiate it from other instances that might be installed on the same computer. It is also easier to identify for deployment.

2. Accept the license agreement by clicking the **I accept the licensing terms and conditions** option.

3. Click the **Next** button. The setup program copies support files that are needed by the setup program itself.

4. Click the **Next** button. The setup program scans your computer for any installed components. If any required components are missing, such as the .NET Framework 2.0, you'll be prompted to install it first. Otherwise, if all tests pass, you'll see a screen like the one shown in Figure 2.1.

Figure 2.1: Passing All Required Setup Tests.

5. Click the **Next** button. The installer inspects your system further.

6. Enter data for the **Name** and **Company** fields.

7. Click the **Next** button.

8. Select from the possible features. To install all features, you need to click the disk icon and select the **Will be installed on local hard drive** option for each option, so that the screen looks like the one shown in Figure 2.2.

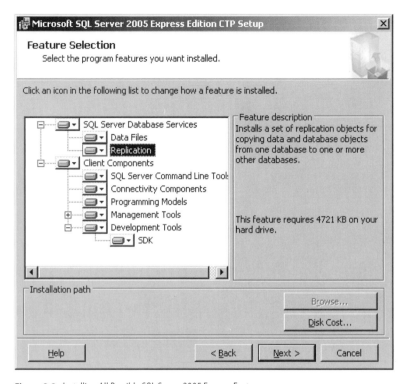

Figure 2.2: Installing All Possible SQL Server 2005 Express Features.

For development purposes, you will likely want to install all services and components.

9. If you wish to change the installation location, click the **Browse** button and change it. By default, your installation will be installed in **C:\Program Files\Microsoft SQL Server**.

10. Click the **Next** button.

11. Select the instance name of your installation. While you can install SQL Server on the default instance, it is not recommended for SQL Server 2005 Express. The recommended instance name for any SQL Server 2005 Express installation is **SQLExpress**, as shown in Figure 2.3. All examples in this book assume this is the instance name. If you wish to see which instances are already installed on your computer, click the **Installed Instances** button.

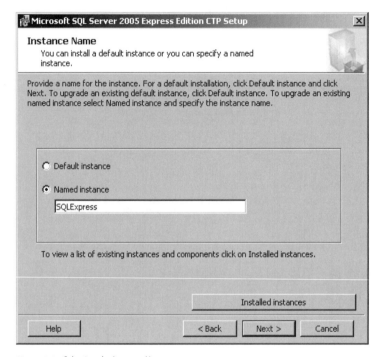

Figure 2.3: Selecting the Instance Name.

12. Click the **Next** button.

13. Select the authentication mode, which is shown in Figure 2.4. Authentication modes are discussed in Chapter 16. If you select the **Mixed Mode** option, you'll also have to enter a password for the system administrator's (**sa**) account. This password should be a complex password, which includes a special character such as **@ or %,** and a number.

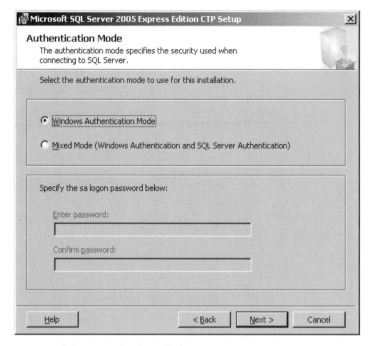

Figure 2.4: Selecting an Authentication Mode.

14. Click the **Next** button.

15. Select **Error and Usage Report** options. If you are installing CTP versions of SQL Server 2005 Express, you can help Microsoft by sending information about how you use SQL Server 2005 Express. These options are selected by default.

16. Click the **Next** button. Read the summary screen.

17. Click the **Install** button to install the options you've selected.

Patching the Installation

For the April CTP version of SQL Server 2005 Express, there was no ability to update the application using the Windows Update Service. However, it is expected by the time the product is released, so you will be able to update SQL Server 2005 Express simply by clicking the **Start⇨ Windows ⇨ Update** menu item.

Uninstalling SQL Server 2005 Express

Before you install a later build of SQL Server 2005 Express, you have to uninstall your current version. To uninstall SQL Server 2005 Express, you use the **Add/Remove Programs** applet from the Windows control panel. Do this by clicking the **Start**⇨ **Settings**⇨ **Control Panel**⇨ **Add or Remove Programs** menu item. You simply uninstall these programs:

▶ Microsoft SQL Server 2005 Express Edition Books Online

▶ Microsoft SQL Server 2005 Express Manager

▶ Microsoft SQL Server 2005 Express Edition

▶ Microsoft SQL Server 2005 Tools Express Edition

▶ Microsoft SQL Native Client

▶ Microsoft SQL Server Setup Support Files

▶ Microsoft Dot Net Framework 2.0 Beta 2

Microsoft also makes an uninstall wizard available for you to use. It is called **sqlbuw.exe**, and is located in the **setup tools\build uninstall wizard** folder under your main setup folder. It will guide you through the process of unistalling a SQL Server 2005 Express build, but may not completely remove a build in all cases. You can always use the **Add/Remove Programs** applet if something goes wrong with the uninstall wizard.

Summary

Because it is a free edition, acquiring SQL Server 2005 Express is very easy. It is available for download, from Microsoft in the form of a CD, or from software vendors. After acquiring the setup programs, installation is quite straightforward.

Installing a Community Technology Preview (CTP) version of SQL Server 2005 is done by using a series of setup programs, with the .NET Framework 2.0 being at the core of those programs. Because the CTP versions are compiled for specific builds of the .NET Framework 2.0, it is important that you uninstall any beta or CTP software before reinstalling a later build. This chapter walked you through the easy process of installing SQL Server 2005 Express from the April CTP.

Chapter 3

SQL Server 2005 Express Tools

SQL Server 2005 Express is much improved over its MSDE predecessor in that visual tools are provided along with the database engine. These tools enable you to manage services, networking protocols, and configurations. The tools also provide the ability to manage databases and their objects, such as tables, views, stored procedures, functions, and more.

This chapter covers the basics of using the tools available in SQL Server 2005 Express. For more information about the networking aspects and considerations for these tools, see Chapters 6 and 9. The examples shown in this chapter use the default instance name of **SQLEXPRESS**. You can change the name of this instance when you install SQL Server 2005 Express, but it is a good idea to leave it as the default to make it obvious that this is not a different edition of SQL Server.

SQL Server Configuration Manager

The SQL Server Configuration Manager is a graphical tool that is automatically installed with SQL Server 2005 Express to enable you to manage many aspects of your SQL Server 2005 installation, such as services, network configuration, and more. Figure 3.1 shows the SQL Server Configuration Manager.

> *Note:*
> The SQL Server Configuration Manager is also used in other editions of SQL Server 2005, but the options and configurations that you will see in those editions can be different than the ones shown in this chapter.

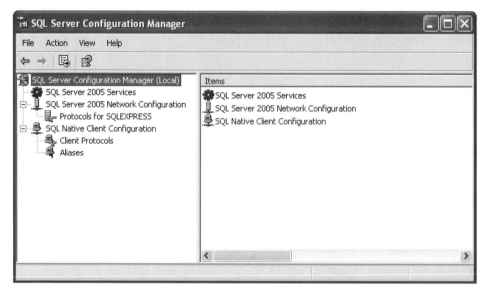

Figure 3.1: SQL Server Configuration Manager for SQL Server 2005 Express.

The SQL Server Configuration Manager displays three main categories of information:

▶ **SQL Server 2005 Services** — Displays a listing of services for your server, such as Analysis Server, SQL Server, and Report Server.

▶ **SQL Server 2005 Network Configuration** — Displays a listing of networking protocols.

▶ **SQL Native Client Configuration** — Displays a listing of configurations for SQL Native Client connections, such as protocols and aliases.

SQL Server 2005 Services

As with all Windows programs that run in the background, SQL Server operates as a set of services. Because SQL Server 2005 Express is a scaled-down edition of SQL Server 2005, not all services are available. The **SQL Server 2005 Services** node in the **SQL Server Configuration Manager** tree is used to list all possible services that are used with SQL Server 2005.

To manage a given service, follow these simple steps:

1. Navigate to the desired service under **the SQL Server 2005 Services** node in the **SQL Server Configuration Manager** tree.

2. Click the desired service. In the right-hand pane, you'll see a list of items for the selected service.

3. Right-click the desired item presented in the right-hand pane and select **Properties** from the drop-down menu. As an example, Figure 3.2 shows the **Advanced** properties available for the **SQLEXPRESS** instance of the **SQL Server** service.

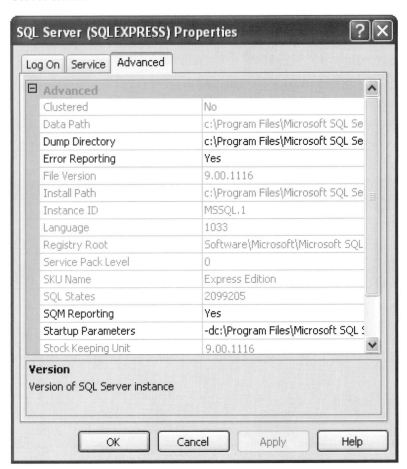

Figure 3.2: SQL Server Service Advanced Properties.

4. Change the desired properties and click the **OK** button to save your changes and close the screen. You can only change these properties:

    ▶ **Dump Directory** — Folder for SQL Server logs.

    ▶ **Error Reporting** — Determines whether errors are transmitted back to Microsoft.

    ▶ **SQM Reporting** — Determines whether reports for service quality are transmitted back to Microsoft. These reports tell Microsoft about the features that are most often used.

    ▶ **Startup Parameters** — Allows you to specify parameters for the SQL Server service.

SQL Server 2005 Network Configuration

The **SQL Server 2005 Network Configuration** node in the **SQL Server Configuration Manager** tree lists the protocols that are to be used to connect to your SQL Server 2005 instance. In SQL Server 2005 Express, there is only one node under **SQL Server 2005 Network Configuration**, which is **Protocols for SQLEXPRESS**. This node is shown in Figure 3.3.

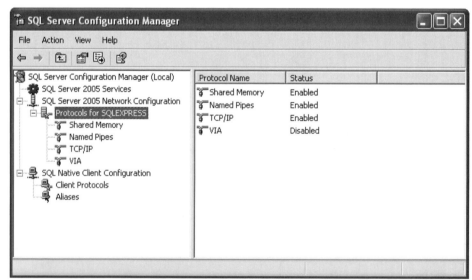

Figure 3.3: Network Configuration Protocols for the SQLEXPRESS Instance.

The default protocols for SQL Server 2005 (including the Express edition) are:

▶ **Shared Memory** — Secure way for a client to access a SQL Server on the same computer. Shared Memory is enabled by default and cannot be used when accessing SQL Server from across the network.

▶ **Named Pipes** — Allows a client to connect to SQL Server by using any of a number of different protocols. The actual protocol used is dictated by the client application by indicating the path, or *pipe*, needed to access the server. Because of potential security risks, only **local Named Pipes** is enabled by default. If you want to use the **Named Pipes** protocol from a remote machine, you'll have to enable this in the **SQL Server Surface Area Configuration** manager, which is shown in Chapter 6.

▶ **TCP/IP** — Standard Ethernet protocol that enables a client application to access a specific SQL Server instance using its IP address. Because of potential security risks, **TCP/IP** is disabled by default.

▶ **VIA** — Stands for Virtual Interface Architecture and is a network protocol that is used in high-speed networks. VIA is not available in SQL Server 2005 Express.

To enable or disable any of the protocols (except VIA), simply right-click the desired protocol name and select **Enable** or **Disable** as desired. If a protocol is enabled, a client application will be able to connect to SQL Server 2005 Express by using that protocol.

SQL Native Client Configuration

SQL Native Client is a new and efficient data access technology that takes advantage of new features in SQL Server 2005. On the other hand, if you are trying to use existing applications that leverage MDAC, you will likely want to upgrade those applications to use the SQL Native Client to gain the advantages of easy distribution. Distribution of SQL Server 2005 Express applications is covered in Chapter 8, while MDAC and SQL Native Client are covered further in Chapter 9.

The **SQL Native Client Configuration** node in the **SQL Server Configuration Manager** tree is used to manage aspects of the SQL Native Client and is broken into two separate nodes in the tree:

► Client Protocols

► Aliases

Client Protocols

The **Client Protocols** node is used to configure the protocols that are to be used to connect to your SQL Server 2005 instance via the SQL Native Client provider. Figure 3.4 shows the **Client Protocols** node under the SQL Native Client Configuration node.

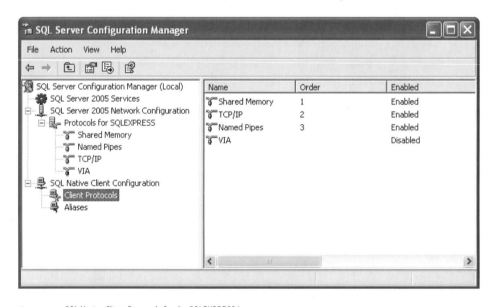

Figure 3.4: SQL Native Client Protocols for the SQLEXPRESS Instance.

These protocols are the same ones listed under the SQL Server 2005 Network Configuration node. Not only do you enable a protocol to be used with the SQL Native Client, but also the order in which the protocol is to take precedence. To manage the protocols used with the SQL Native Client, follow these easy steps:

1. Right-click the **Client Protocols** node.

2. Select **Properties** from the drop-down menu. This will bring up the screen shown in Figure 3.5.

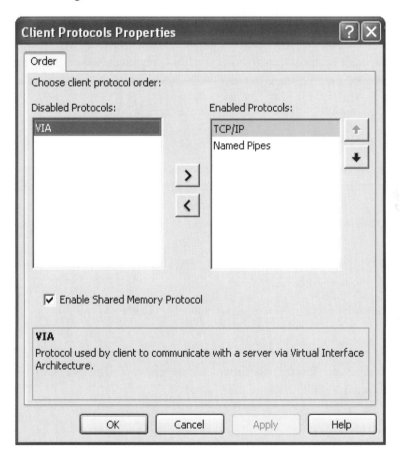

Figure 3.5: Client Protocols Properties.

3. Enable a protocol by selecting the desired item in the **Disabled Protocols** box and clicking the > button. This will move the protocol from the **Disabled Protocols** box to the **Enabled Protocols** box. The only exception is if you want to enable the **Shared Memory** protocol. If you do, simply ensure the **Enable Shared Memory Protocol** check box is selected.

4.   Disable a protocol by selecting the desired item in the **Enabled Protocols** box and clicking the < button. This will move the protocol from the **Enabled Protocols** box to the **Disabled Protocols** box.

5.   To configure the precedence of a protocol, select the desired item in the **Enabled Protocols** box and click the ↑ or ↓ buttons as desired. The order in which the protocols are shown is the order of precedence.

6.   Click the **OK** button to save your changes and close the screen.

Aliases

An *alias* is user-friendly way to specify and configure all the properties required by a protocol to make a connection to SQL Server when using the SQL Native Client. For example, if you have a production server named **SERV01** and you wish to connect via TCP/IP, you might configure an alias that is named **Prod** and specify the server name or IP address, along with the port to use for connection to the server. Then, your application needs only to reference the name **Prod** in its connection. The **Aliases** node is used to configure these aliases for use with your SQL Native Client connections.

To create a new SQL Native Client alias, follow these easy steps:

1.   Right-click the **Aliases** node.

2.   Select **New Alias** from the drop-down menu. This will bring up the screen shown in Figure 3.6.

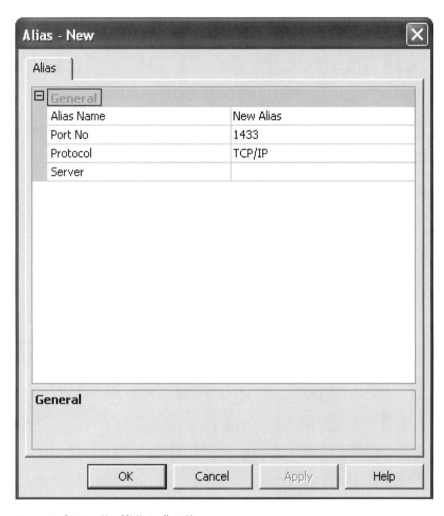

Figure 3.6: Creating a New SQL Native Client Alias.

3. Enter the desired **Alias Name**. This name will be used to make the connection.

4. Enter the **Port No** for the TCP/IP address on which the desired instance will listen. If you selected **Named Pipes** as the protocol, you must enter the pipe name.

5. Select the desired **Protocol** from the drop-down list. **TCP/IP** is selected by default.

6. Enter the desired Server, which can be the name of your server or its IP address.

7. Click the **OK** button to save your changes and close the screen.

Express Manager

Express Manager, sometimes known as XM, is a tool that lets you graphically manage the objects in your SQL Server 2005 Express instance. These objects include databases, tables, views, stored procedures, and more. XM also lets you issue queries against a database by using the built-in Query Editor.

Note:

In the XM Preview, there is limited support for actually managing objects. Instead, most objects can only be viewed if they have been created using SQL. An exception is the ability to create and delete databases directly from within XM.

Figure 3.7 shows how the Express Manager looks, although your configuration will be completely dependent on the objects that exist on your server.

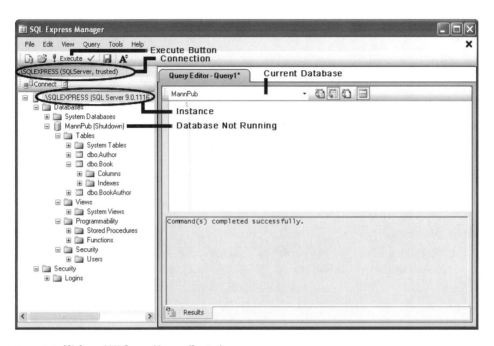

Figure 3.7: SQL Server 2005 Express Manager (Preview).

There are a few things to notice in Figure 3.7 besides the hierarchical object structure of each database. The first is the connection information at the top of the screen. Figure 3.7 shows that this connection to the **SQLEXPRESS** instance is made by using a trusted (Windows) connection. Figure 3.7 also shows the instance name at the top of the tree from which all objects are displayed. It also shows the version of the instance. For each of the databases, it is also shown if the database is not running. If the database is not running, you'll see the word (**Shutdown**) after the name of the database. A database that is shut down means that no users are connected to it and it is effectively detached from the SQL Server instance. Likewise, the instance will automatically start when a user connects to it. Finally, the query window on the right-hand part of the screen shows the database that is currently in use within the SQL Server instance. This is very similar to the way the SQL Server Query Analyzer works in SQL Server 2000. The Query Editor lets you type SQL statements, execute them, and return results.

SQLCMD

SQLCMD is a command-line tool for issuing commands against a SQL Server 2005 instance without the need for any graphical tools. SQLCMD can connect (using the **–A** parameter) to a SQL Server 2005 instance using a dedicated administrative connection so that any commands that you issue will not be hampered by slow performance on your server. SQLCMD issues commands in batches, so it prompts you for each line in the batch with a line number. When you are finished entering each line in your batch, enter the **GO** keyword and your batch will be executed.

Note:

SQLCMD is not case-sensitive. It is only capitalized in this chapter for emphasis.

SQLCMD can be a little complex to use because there are so many connection options, but here are the basics of how you use SQLCMD:

1. Open a command prompt by clicking the **Start⇨ Programs⇨ Accessories ⇨ Command Prompt** menu item. Alternatively, you could simply click the **Start⇨ Run** menu item and type cmd (which stands for Command Prompt), and press the **Enter** key.

2. Run the SQLCMD program. When you run the program, you establish a connection between your console and a SQL Server 2005 instance (including the Express edition). Here are the basics of creating a connection:

SYNTAX (Connecting with SQL Server security)
```
sqlcmd -S <server>\<instance> -U <username> -P <password>
```

EXAMPLE
```
sqlcmd -S Prod01\SQLExpress -U sqladmin -P 12345
```

SYNTAX (Connecting with Windows security)
```
sqlcmd -S <server>\<instance>
```

EXAMPLE
```
sqlcmd -S Prod01\SQLExpress
```

In Example 1 and Example 2, a connection is established with an instance named **SQLExpress** on the computer named **Prod01**. Example 1, because it uses SQL Server security, connects with a user name of **sqladmin** and a password of **12345**. Example 2 connects using Windows security, so no user name or password is required. The current network login is used.

Tech Tip:
You don't need to specify the server name if you are running SQLCMD on the same machine as the instance is installed. Instead, you simply use the dot "." notation, such as .\SQLExpress.

You'll see the SQLCMD program running, which is shown in Figure 3.8.

Figure 3.8: SQLCMD Program.

After you login to SQL Server 2005 using SQLCMD, you will see a command prompt beginning with the current line number in the batch. This is very similar to what you see in the Query Editor of the Express Manager. You can begin entering valid commands, such as SQL or operating system commands. You can select data from the database, kill all connections, start processes, run stored procedures, and perform virtually any other task that can be run by issuing a command. To find out what commands are available through SQLCMD, you can refer to SQL Server Books Online (BOL) or issue the **:help** command (followed by pressing the **Enter** key). This displays a list of commands, as shown in Figure 3.9.

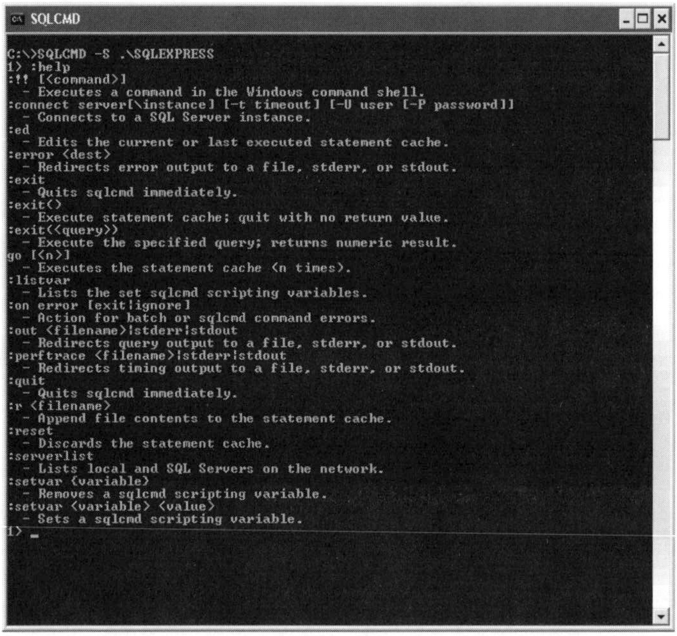

Figure 3.9: SQLCMD :help Command.

Summary

SQL Server 2005 Express includes useful tools for managing services, networking protocols, configurations, and more.

The SQL Server Configuration Manager tool contains a **SQL Server 2005 Services** node (which lists services for your server), a **SQL Server 2005 Network Configuration** node (which lists networking configurations), and a **SQL Native Client Configuration** node (which lists configurations for SQL Native Client connections).

Another tool is Express Manager, or XM, which lets you graphically manage the objects in a SQL Server Express 2005 instance, such as databases, tables, views, stored procedures, and more.

The SQLCMD tool allows you to use the command line to issue commands against a SQL Server 2005 instance. It also allows a dedicated administrative connection, so that your commands are not affected by slow server performance.

Chapter 4

Common Language Runtime

From the very first release of the Microsoft .NET Framework, it supported the concept of the Common Language Runtime, or CLR. In fact, it is one of the major architectural designs of .NET. The concept being that Microsoft provides a set of base libraries, or classes, which will support common services to all .NET applications, regardless of the computer language in which they are written, or the type of application that is being built. The types of .NET applications that can benefit from CLR include (but are not limited to):

- ▶ Windows applications

- ▶ Class libraries

- ▶ Mobile applications

- ▶ Web applications

- ▶ Web services

- ▶ Console applications

Prior to the release of SQL Server 2005 (any edition), there was no correlation between any applications or libraries written in a .NET language except that they may have connected to a SQL Server database. However, with SQL Server 2005, there is a deep integration of the database with the core services of .NET. This integration is known as CLR integration. This chapter discusses the overall concept of CLR, the .NET Framework, and what they mean for your SQL Server 2005 Express installations.

CLR Advantages

Prior to SQL Server 2005, there was limited support for some types of operations that were typically done in other languages (Visual Basic, C#, C++, etc.), such as complex computing algorithms. Some of these types of operations could be done in Transact-SQL, but this is not what it was designed for. However, there was little or no choice because of the limitations of SQL Server 2000 and earlier versions. Now, with SQL Server 2005 and CLR integration, you can write high-performance .NET code, compile it into an assembly, and host the assembly inside SQL Server 2005. SQL Server supports hosting CLR assemblies for these types of SQL Server objects:

▶ **Stored procedures** – Covered in Chapter 11.

▶ **Triggers** – Covered in Chapter 13.

▶ **User-defined types** – Covered in Chapter 14.

▶ **User-defined functions** – Covered in Chapter 14.

There are many advantages in using CLR (.NET) assemblies. First of all, .NET assemblies are referred to as *managed code*. Managed code is controlled by the .NET Framework. This is an advantage because your managed applications have automatic garbage collection, type checking at runtime, a built-in security model, preemptive threading, and more. This means that you can be assured that even poorly designed or coded assemblies that someone else develops won't have an adverse reaction to your assemblies.

.NET assemblies can be written in any language supported by the .NET runtime, including:

▶ Visual Basic

▶ Visual C#

▶ Visual C++

▶ Visual J++

▶ COBOL

The following discussion of how .NET assemblies are compiled is illustrated by Figure 4.1.

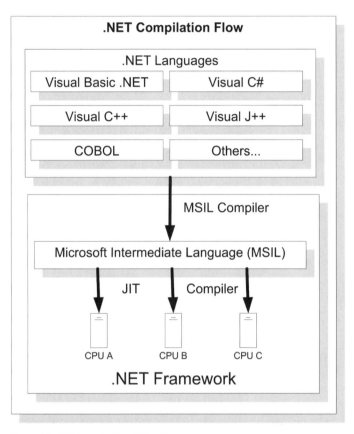

Figure 4.1: .NET Assembly Compilation Flow.

Code needs to execute at the CPU level in machine instructions. However, there are many different types of CPUs, each with its own set of capabilities and instruction sets. Therefore, when you compile your .NET code into an assembly, it compiles not to the machine level, but to a level just high enough where any language can be compiled for use by any machine, regardless of its CPU. This is known as Microsoft Intermediate Language, or *MSIL*. This way, the MSIL code is completely portable and CPU-independent. MSIL code can be run on any machine, because the .NET Framework takes care of further compiling and running the MSIL code at runtime, based on the type of CPU that has to execute the code. When MSIL code is compiled for a specific CPU, it is compiled in a process called just-in-time (or JIT) compiling because it is done on the fly.

CLR and SQL Server 2005

Creating SQL Server 2005 objects (stored procedures, triggers, user-defined types, and user-defined functions) using the .NET language of your choice is only as difficult as your requirements dictate. You can have a simple "Hello World" function that takes one minute to develop, or you can be working on your .NET code for weeks or months. It all depends (as is the answer to virtually any IT question) on the complexity required. However, the concept of what you do to get your .NET assemblies hosted inside SQL Server is the same. The process follows these basic steps:

1. Create your .NET assembly, but do so by indicating that the *methods* that you declare inside a *class* will not modify any state information of the class and are not associated with a specific instance of a class. This is done in C# .NET with the **static** keyword and in Visual Basic .NET with the **shared** keyword. You must write your .NET assemblies to target the same version of the .NET Framework that SQL Server 2005 supports. The easiest way to do this is to use a corresponding version of Visual Studio 2005. See "Visual Studio 2005" later in this chapter for more information.

2. The assembly containing any number of classes and methods is compiled into a .NET assembly.

3. The assembly is uploaded into SQL Server by using the **CREATE ASSEMBLY** Transact-SQL statement. At this point, the .NET assembly is actually copied into the database so that it can be portable. Another advantage of copying the assembly into the database is that it is now a snapshot of your code and is not affected if you recompile your assembly (and possibly break any interface required by your SQL Server objects).

4. Your SQL Server objects are created by using the **CREATE** *<object>* Transact-SQL statement, where *<object>* is either **PROCEDURE, FUNCTION, TRIGGER, TYPE**, or **AGGREGATE**, depending on the type of object you're trying to create. For more information on these functions, see their respective chapters in this book.

5. You reference the object in Transact-SQL code as if it was a native object. For example, it will be completely transparent if you execute the **usp_ CalculateSales** stored procedure written in a CLR language vs. the **usp_ GetData** stored procedure written in Transact-SQL.

CLR Scenarios

To help understand the concept of CLR integration, it is probably best to look at some scenarios that are good candidates for using CLR assemblies. While there is no "be-all, end-all" rule to know when you would write something in CLR vs. Transact-SQL, there are some guidelines to help you, which are outlined in Table 4.1

Scenario	CLR	Transact-SQL
Any "set-based" queries against a database		X
Code for business logic layer (middle-tier)	X	
Code for high volume data retrieval		X
Complex algorithms based on data		X
Complex algorithms based on logic	X	
General data access (insert, update, delete)		X
Logic based on need to determine which Windows users and groups a user belongs to (if GroupA, then perform one action, if GroupB, then perform a different action)	X	
Logic that relies on SQL Server to manage access to data and objects (either with Windows or SQL Server security)		X
Operations that call existing assemblies	X	
Procedural logic	X	

Table 4.1: CLR vs. Transact-SQL Guidelines.

The scenarios in Table 4.1 are a broad set of rules. Certainly individual factors may influence the decision of whether to use CLR or Transact-SQL, but it does show the general guidelines that you should consider.

As an example, suppose you are a mortgage broker and you need to provide scenarios to prospective clients. These scenarios are based on lots of factors, such as interest rates, type of mortgage, term length, down payment, refinance or new mortgage, and many others. These types of complex calculations should be done in .NET code, not in Transact-SQL.

Another example from Table 4.1 is the scenario where you need to run a report based on summarizing data in tables that contain a large amount of data. Suppose you have a **SalesHistory** table that contains 10 million rows of data. You're certainly not going to return all that data into .NET code. You want to let the powerful engine inside SQL Server do what it is best at, which is querying data.

 Caution:

The ability to write CLR code in SQL Server 2005, while very useful, can arm you with the tools for doing the wrong thing. The most common error in CLR stored procedures is using procedural logic where set-based logic should be used. Sometimes it's easier to select every row in a table and increment through each row one at a time until you find what you are looking for, rather than to figure out a way to write a complex SQL statement to perform the operation better, faster, and with less system resources. The problem really surfaces when you have lots of data. Anything will perform well when retrieving only 50 rows. Use caution when determining whether to use Transact-SQL or CLR stored procedures.

Then there are cases where it is not clear whether to use Transact-SQL or CLR. For example, suppose you need to calculate discounts on software that you sell, based on the following rules:

▶ Whether a contract is in place at a pre-negotiated discount

▶ Volume commitment in the contract

▶ Site license or per-seat licenses

These rules are simple enough that they probably don't use complex logic, and may require only a simple calculation based on data values retrieved in a table. Therefore, it would probably be just a matter of choice whether to implement this calculation in CLR or Transact-SQL. On the other hand, if your organization is building a business logic layer that contains logic and rules used for the entire company, it probably makes sense to write the rules in .NET logic, so that your code base for the logic can be used either in the database or external assemblies that might be called from a Web page or another application.

 Caution:

Remember that .NET assemblies are copied into the database with the **CREATE DATABASE** Transact-SQL statement. If you use the same code base to compile assemblies that are used inside and outside the database, you have to implement a process to ensure that if you update your code, you not only compile the assembly and deploy it into your business logic layer, but also into the database. It's very easy to do, but it's important for you to know that these are two separate steps.

Enabling CLR Integration

Before you can use CLR integration (aka .NET assemblies) with SQL Server 2005 Express, you have to enable it in the engine. In an effort to reduce the surface area of the server that is exposed to the outside world, CLR integration is turned off by default. To enable CLR integration, follow these simple steps:

1. Launch the Surface Area Configuration Manager by clicking the **Start ⇨ Programs ⇨ Microsoft SQL Server 2005 CTP ⇨ Configuration Tools ⇨ SQL Server Surface Area Configuration** menu item.

2. Select the **Surface Area Configuration for Features** link.

3. Click the **CLR Integration** node in the tree.

4. Ensure that the **Enable CLR Integration** option is checked, as shown in Figure 4.2.

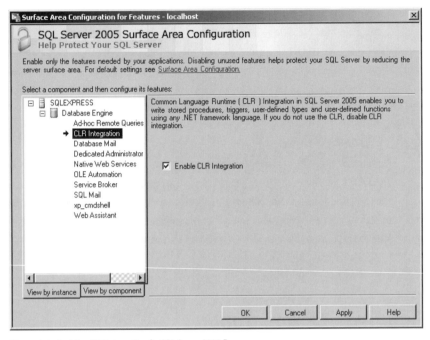

Figure 4.2: Enabling CLR Integration for SQL Server 2005 Express.

5. Click the **OK** button to save your changes and close the screen. Your SQL Server installation is now configured to host CLR integration.

Once you have enabled CLR integration, you can deploy your assemblies into the database and use the CLR functions described throughout this book to use the assemblies.

Visual Studio 2005

Because SQL Server 2005 is so tightly integrated with the CLR, the version of the .NET Framework and the version of Visual Studio 2005 must be in sync. Visual Studio 2005 and all its different "flavors," such as Visual Studio 2005 Express and Visual Web Developer 2005 Express, use not only the same version of the .NET Framework, but also the same build number. For example, Visual Studio 2005 Express Beta 2 uses build 2.0.50215 of the .NET Framework, as does the April CTP version of SQL Server 2005 Express. To learn more about the Visual Studio 2005 environment, see Chapter 5.

Microsoft distributes the .NET Framework as a downloadable file named dotnetfx.exe. If you want to know what build number the framework is, you can follow these simple steps:

1. Locate and right-click the **dotnetfx.exe** file.

2. Select the **Properties** item from the pop-up menu.

3. Click the **Version** tab.

4. Click the **File Version** item in the **Item name** list. The **Value** field shows the version number.

That's how you know the version of the .NET Framework. A centralized place to find downloadable versions of the .NET Framework is on the Microsoft Web site at `http://msdn.microsoft.com/netframework/downloads/updates`.

Tech Tip:
You may want to rename the executable file from **dotnetfx.exe** to include the version number, such as **dotnetfx_v2.0.50215.exe**, if you are going to keep multiple versions of the .NET Framework redistributable around. This makes it very easy to locate the correct version that you need.

Summary

Microsoft's decision to host CLR assemblies inside SQL Server 2005 greatly enhances the capabilities and performance of SQL Server. Prior versions of SQL Server had limited support for calling a procedure outside SQL Server. In SQL Server 2005, the CLR is tightly integrated to enable you to create high-performance .NET code that can be used in stored procedures, triggers, user-defined types, and user-defined functions.

The use of CLR in the database is very easy, but is turned off by default. You must use the Surface Area Configuration Manager to turn it on. Once you do, you can use any of the Visual Studio 2005 products to write CLR stored procedures, triggers, user-defined types, and user-defined functions. For more information on actually writing CLR objects, refer to the chapters in this book that correspond to the type of object you would like to create. For more information about Visual Studio 2005, see Chapter 5.

Did you know?

.NET assemblies are compiled in Visual Studio 2005 in the folder structure under a project. However, these assemblies can be stored in a common place where all Windows applications can access them. This location is called the Global Assembly Cache, or GAC.

Visual Studio 2005

Visual Studio 2005 is a software development environment that is tightly integrated into SQL Server 2005. In fact, each Visual Studio 2005 edition comes with SQL Server 2005 Express. Visual Studio 2005 is used to develop Web-based applications, Windows applications, class libraries, mobile applications, and more. It comes in these"flavors:"

► **Visual Studio 2005 Express Edition** — Enables hobbyists and students to develop basic applications for their own use and includes support for developing CLR assemblies that can be hosted in SQL Server 2005. These products are further categorized into two separate products:

- **Visual Web Developer 2005 Express** — Designed to enable software development specifically for Web applications in your choice of .NET languages.

- **Visual Basic 2005 Express** — Designed to enable software development using the Visual Basic .NET language.

► **Visual Studio 2005 Standard Edition** — Builds upon the Express edition and allows you to develop different types of applications suitable for a department or small company. It includes support for SQL Server 2005 Reporting Services.

► **Visual Studio 2005 Professional Edition** — Builds upon the Standard edition to include remote debugging and more SQL Server 2005 tools.

► **Visual Studio 2005 Team System** — Builds upon the Professional edition and is designed for use by software development teams. This edition includes the Developer Edition of SQL Server 2005.

There are many useful and productive things that you can do with Visual Studio 2005. For example, you can connect to a SQL Server 2005 Express database and manage its objects. You can create new tables, views, stored procedures, and more. Because of the tight integration with SQL Server 2005 Express, Visual Studio 2005 even lets you even lets you debug stored procedures by stepping through them line-by-line to see how they perform. This chapter describes the basics of using Visual Studio 2005 to prepare you for using it with SQL Server 2005 Express.

Note:

This chapter was written using Visual Basic 2005 language from the Beta 2 version of Visual Studio 2005 Professional, which also installs the April CTP version of SQL Server 2005 Express.

Before diving into this chapter, take a look at Figure 5.1, which shows the Visual Studio 2005 Integrated Development Environment, or IDE. Figure 5.1 is the basis for all other discussions in this chapter.

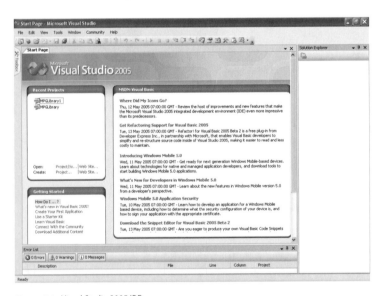

Figure 5.1: Visual Studio 2005 IDE.

Creating Projects

All code in Visual Studio 2005 is contained within a project. Therefore, if you are going to use Visual Studio 2005 to create a library of code that can be used within SQL Server 2005 Express, you first create a project. To create a project, follow these steps:

1. Click the **File⇨New Project** menu item. This brings up the screen shown in Figure 5.2, which lets you choose the type of project to create.

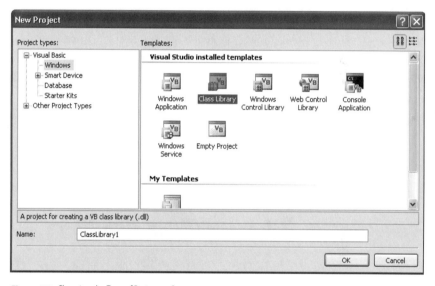

Figure 5.2: Choosing the Type of Project to Create.

2. To create CLR objects within SQL Server 2005 Express, click the **Class Library** template.

3. Enter the name of your library. Choose this name carefully, as it will result in the name of your DLL file that is compiled. It can be changed later, but it's easier just to name it appropriately at this time. For example, **MPGLibrary** is the name of the library used for my company (Mann Publishing Group).

4. Click the **OK** button. A new class file is created, associated with the new project, and opened.

5. Enter code into the class file according to the directions shown in the various chapters throughout this book. You can certainly create additional classes and compile them into the same assembly if you wish.

Compiling Assemblies

Once you enter your code according to the instructions found throughout this book, you are ready to compile your project into a .NET assembly. To compile the assembly, simply click the **Build⇨Build <ProjectName>** menu item, where *ProjectName* is the name of the project that you created earlier in this chapter For the project named **MPGLibrary**, for example, the menu item is **Build⇨Build MPGLibrary**. This compiles a DLL file, which is now a .NET assembly that can be registered in SQL Server 2005 using the **CREATE ASSEMBLY** Transact-SQL statement.

.NET assemblies are, by default, compiled into the **My Documents\Visual Studio 2005\Projects\<ProjectName>\<ProjectName>\bin\Release** folder. For example, the MPGLibrary project described earlier is compiled into the **My Documents\Visual Studio 2005\Projects\MPGLibrary\MPGLibrary\bin\Release** folder and named **MPGLibrary.dll**. These names and locations are used when creating the assembly inside SQL Server 2005. The **CREATE ASSEMBLY** Transact-SQL statement is discussed in Chapter 11, which shows how to use it for CLR stored procedures. However, registering the assembly in SQL Server 2005 Express follows the same procedure, regardless of the type of CLR object you are hosting.

Connecting to SQL Server 2005 Databases

The Visual Studio 2005 IDE lets you connect to all editions of SQL Server 2005 databases, including the Express edition. Once connected, you can manage the objects on the server, including databases and the objects contained within those databases. To connect to SQL Server, open your Visual Studio 2005 project and follow these steps:

1. Click the **View⇨Server Explorer** menu item.

2. Click the **Connect to Database** button (the third button from the left). This brings up the screen shown in Figure 5.3.

Figure 5.3: Creating a New SQL Server Connection.

3. Ensure the Data source reads **Microsoft SQL Server (SqlClient)**, as it should by default.

4. Enter or select the desired server in the Server name box. Make sure you follow the *Server\Instance* format. For example, to connect to the local computer's SQLEXPRESS instance, enter `.\SQLEXPRESS` (with **.** indicating the local server).

5. Choose the desired authentication mode in the **Log on to the server** section of the screen.

6. Enter or select the name of the desired database in the **Select or enter a database name** box.

7. Click the **Test Connection** button to test your connection. If you receive any error messages, correct the parameters selected on the screen and try it again before you continue.

8. Click the **OK** button. Your database and server are now connected to Visual Studio 2005. In the **Server Explorer** window, you'll see the active

connection, as well as any objects that exist on the server (if you expand the object container in the tree). This new connection is shown in Figure 5.4.

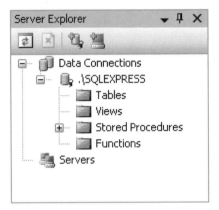

Figure 5.4: New Data Connection.

Once you are connected to a SQL Server 2005 Express database, you can manage its objects by right-clicking on any of the objects and selecting the desired action. For example, you can right-click the **Data Connections** item and create a new database. Likewise, you can expand **Stored Procedures** to list all of the stored procedures that exist on the server. Not only does Visual Studio 2005 show a listing of the stored procedures, but you can perform these actions:

▶ Create new stored procedure.

▶ Open an existing stored procedure, which lets you edit it.

▶ Execute the stored procedure. If it expects any parameters, you will be prompted for values for those parameters.

▶ Step into the stored procedure. Again, if the stored procedure expects any parameters, you will be prompted for values for those parameters. Those parameters are used when stepping through the stored procedure.

Including Database Connections in Your Projects

The last section showed you how to explore your database server and manage its databases and database objects. However, just because you managed the server does not mean that a database is included in your project. To include a SQL Server Express 2005 database as a data source in a Visual Studio 2005 project, follow these simple steps:

1. In the **Solution Explorer** pane, right-click the name of your project and select the **Add⇨Existing Item** item from the pop-up menu.

2. In the dialog box presented, select **Data Files** from the **Files of type** drop-down list. This will filter the types of files shown to include database **.mdf** files.

3. Navigate to the desired **.mdf** file.

4. Click the **Add** button. This adds the selected SQL Server Express file to the project.

> ### Note:
> The database file that you select is copied into your Visual Studio 2005 project folder.

5. The database file is now added to the project and will be listed in the Server Explorer window as a data connection. You may have to click the **Refresh** button if you don't see your new data source.

When you add a database file to the project, it is added to the project with the **User Instance = true** parameter added to the connection string. To verify this, in the Server Explorer, right-click the desired connection and click the **Modify Connection** item from the pop-up menu. Clicking the **Advanced** button shows the screen in Figure 5.5.

Figure 5.5: Advanced Connection Properties.

From this point, you can use the database connection in your application, which is beyond the scope of this book. However, to whet your appetite, Figure 5.6 shows a sample application that uses the new SQL Server 2005 Express data connection in a data source whose fields are bound to a form for easy updating. This simple application took less than five minutes to create.

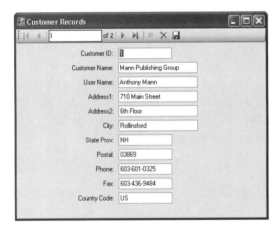

Figure 5.6: Sample Visual Studio 2005 Application Using a SQL Server 2005 Express Connection.

Summary

Visual Studio 2005, with all its different editions, incorporates tight integration with SQL Server 2005 Express. Not only can you use Visual Studio 2005 to create .NET assemblies that can be used with SQL Server 2005 Express CLR objects, but also to manage the database server itself. You can use the Server Explorer to view and manage your SQL Server objects on any SQL Server 2005 edition by using the SQL Native Client. You can also include a database **.mdf** file in your Visual Studio 2005 projects, which automatically sets the **User Instance** = **true** attribute of the connection string. This chapter outlined how to perform all of these actions from within the Visual Studio 2005 environment.

Did you know?

Unlike the Express edition of SQL Server 2005, the Express edition of Visual Basic 2005 is not free. Microsoft plans to release it for under $50 US.

Administration

Chapter 6

Configuration

You have probably heard of Microsoft mentioning that its products are "secure by default." This means that without doing any additional configuration, the installation or setup program for a given product will make it as secure as possible. The same is true for SQL Server 2005 Express.

By default, SQL Server 2005 Express is configured as follows:

▶ All SQL Server-related services are turned off.

▶ All network protocols are disabled.

▶ Most database engine features are disabled or turned off.

By default, if everything is turned on, enabled, and running, you could expose your SQL Server to potential attacks. In other words, the surface area of your SQL Server would be large. Therefore, when SQL Server 2005 is secure by default, the surface area is small. You can think of this concept as if it was a B2 bomber. Without its stealth features, it is a large airplane with a big surface area. On the other hand, with its stealth features, it appears to the outside world as if it has little or no surface area. The same is true for SQL Server, depending on which features are turned on or enabled. It is a good idea to turn off any feature that you don't use.

To shrink or enlarge the surface area of your SQL Server, you use a tool called the SQL Server 2005 Surface Area Configuration Wizard. This chapter shows how to use this wizard to manage the networking configuration of SQL Server 2005 Express, and also how to understand the networking issues surrounding this product.

SQL Server 2005 Surface Area Configuration Wizard

The SQL Server 2005 Surface Area Configuration Wizard is used to manage the services and features that are exposed to the outside world. To launch this wizard, click the **Start**⇨ **Programs**⇨ **Microsoft SQL Server 2005 CTP**⇨ **Configuration Tools**⇨ **SQL Server Surface Area Configuration** menu item. When you do, you'll be presented with a choice of the type of surface area to configure, as follows:

► **Surface Area Configuration for Services and Connections** — Used to manage the services accounts for SQL Server 2005 Express and its remote connections.

► **Surface Area Configuration for Features** — Used to manage which features are enabled within SQL Server 2005 Express.

To select an area to configure, simply click the desired link and the selected configuration area will be shown in a new screen.

Surface Area Configuration for Services and Connections

The **Surface Area Configuration for Services and Connections** screen lets you configure database engine parameters. By default, when you enter this screen, you'll be configuring parameters of the **SQLExpress** services, as shown in Figure 6.1.

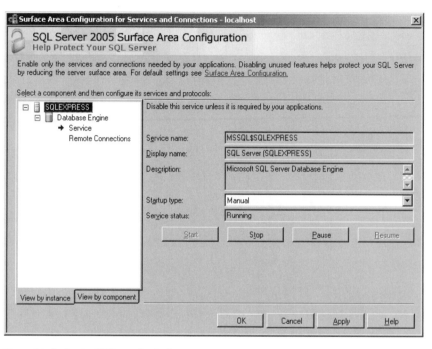

Figure 6.1: Configuring SQLExpress Service Parameters.

When you install SQL Server 2005 Express, the service is set to a **Startup type** of **Manual**. This means that you will not be able to connect to SQL Server 2005 Express unless you start the service or change the **Startup type** property. If you plan to do anything in SQL Server 2005 Express, you'll need to start the service by clicking the **Start** button. If you want SQL Server 2005 Express to run automatically after you reboot your computer, then you should also change the **Startup type** property to **Automatic** and click the **Apply** button to save your changes.

Click the **Remote Connections** node in the tree on the left-hand part of the screen to configure remote connections. Doing so shows the screen shown in Figure 6.2.

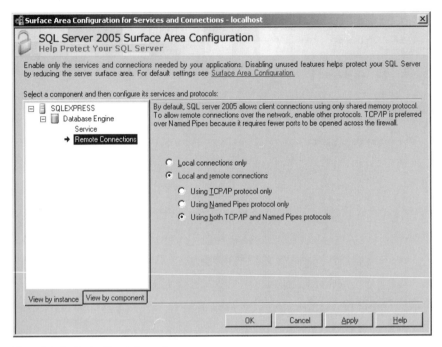

Figure 6.2: Configuring Remote Connections.

Select one of the following options:

▶ **Local connections only** — Disallows remote connections. Local connections will be made using shared memory or local named pipes. If you are using SQL Server 2005 Express from a local application, this option is likely the desired one.

▶ **Local and remote connections** — Allows not only local connections using shared memory, but also remote connections by using the protocol selected below.

▶ **Using TCP/IP protocol only** — Connect using only the TCP/IP protocol. This is the most likely option to select if remote connections are to be made to SQL Server 2005 Express.

▶ **Using Named Pipes protocol only** — Connect using only the Named Pipes protocol. Named Pipes provides a little more flexibility over TCP/IP because it requires less configuration, but needs more ports open in your firewall than does TCP/IP.

▶ **Using both TCP/IP and Named Pipes protocols** — Connect using TCP/IP and Named Pipes, allowing for many different scenarios to connect to SQL Server 2005 Express.

After making your changes, click the **OK** button to save your changes and close the screen.

Surface Area Configuration for Features

The **Surface Area Configuration for Features** screen lets you configure database engine features. For each feature that you will use, make sure it is enabled, but make sure to disable any feature that you don't want to use, because it enlarges the surface area of your SQL Server. The **Surface Area Configuration for Features** screen is shown in Figure 6.3.

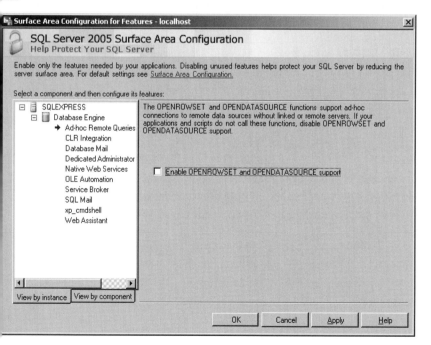

Figure 6.3: Configuring SQL Server Express Features.

By clicking the desired feature name listed in the node in the tree, you can configure these features:

▶ **Ad-hoc Remote Queries** — Configures the ability of applications to make ad-hoc queries to your server instance without needing them to configure your instance as a linked server. There is a single option under this node, which is **Enable OPENROWSET and OPENDATASOURCE support**. By default, this option is not selected, but you can select it if your remote application needs to use either of these functions.

▶ **CLR Integration** — Configures the use of .NET Common Language Runtime (CLR) support. There is a single option under this node, called **Enable CLR Integration**. Many chapters in this book show how to create SQL Server objects using CLR. By default, this option is not selected, but if you wish to use CLR, you must select this option.

▶ **Database Mail** — Configures the ability to send e-mail from your SQL Server. A single option under this node, called **Enable Database Mail stored procedures**, is not selected by default. However, if your server needs to send e-mail, select this option.

▶ **Dedicated Administrator** — Configures the use of remote connections to your SQL Server instance via a Dedicated Administrative Connection (DAC), much the way SQLCMD does. Unfortunately DAC is not available in the Express edition of SQL Server 2005 and thus is not covered in this book.

▶ **Native Web Services** — Configures the HTTP endpoints available to SQL Server 2005 to access Web Services by using HTTP/SOAP. Unfortunately Native Web Services and HTTP endpoints are not available in the Express edition of SQL Server 2005 and thus are not covered in this book.

▶ **OLE Automation** — Configures the ability to use OLE Automation to use external OLE Automation (OA) objects, such as COM objects via any stored procedure whose name is prefixed with **sp_oa**. By default, the **Enable OLE Automation** option under this node is disabled, but you can enable it if you need OLE Automation. With the new features of SQL Server 2005 Express, it is unlikely that you need this option enabled unless you need to support legacy code.

▶ **Service Broker** — Configures the endpoints available to SQL Server for Service Broker applications. Some additional information about Service Broker applications is available in Chapter 17.

> *Note:*
>
> For in-depth coverage of how to create and implement Service Broker applications, **see** *The Rational Guide to SQL Server 2005 Service Broker Beta Preview,* **by Roger Wolter, published by Rational Press, ISBN 1-932577-20-3.**

▶ **SQL Mail** — This option is similar to the **Database Mail** option, but uses an older technology available in SQL Server 2000. Unless your applications use legacy code that sends SQL Mail, you should leave the **Enable SQL Mail stored procedures** option under this node disabled and use database mail instead.

▶ **xp_cmdshell** — Configures the ability to execute operating system commands using the xp_cmdshell extended stored procedure. Selecting the **Enable xp_cmdshell** option under this node should only be done if necessary, as it poses a potential significant security risk.

▶ **Web Assistant** — Configures the use of special stored procedures that generate HTML code. The **Enable Web Assistant** option under this node should only be enabled if legacy code needs to use these special stored procedures.

After changing any option under one of the nodes listed above, click the **OK** button to save your changes and close the screen.

TCP/IP Remote Ports

Even if you have enabled remote connections (see "Surface Area Configuration for Services and Connections" earlier in this chapter), you'll have to make sure that your firewall isn't going to block the TCP/IP traffic from reaching the SQL Server.

In general, there are two ways to make TCP/IP connections to your SQL Server:

1. By manually specifying a specific connection port on which SQL Server listens. This option is not available for SQL Server 2005 Express Manager connections.

2. By broadcasting connection requests to the SQL Browser service, which, in turn, "finds" the port on which SQL Server listens. Of course, if the SQL Browser service is not running, this method will not work. This option is available for SQL Server 2005 Express Manager connections and connections from applications, such as those created with any version of Visual Studio.

To illustrate how ports work, let's discuss how to configure your system to connect with SQL Server 2005 Express Manager (XM). If you want to see how to connect to a remote server using any version of Visual Studio, see Chapter 5.

When you use XM to connect to a SQL Server 2005 Express database, you cannot specify a specific TCP/IP port, so it uses the SQL Browser service to determine on which ports your SQL Server 2005 Express database is listening. Therefore, before you can make any connections, you have to configure SQL Server 2005 Express to listen for TCP/IP connections and also to open the required ports in the firewall.

Tech Tip:
If you are running SQL Server 2005 Express on Windows XP with Service Pack 2 (SP2) installed, you will likely encounter problems connecting to the database, unless you explicitly follow the procedures described herein.

To configure SQL Server 2005 Express to accept remote connections, follow these instructions carefully:

1. Open the SQL Configuration Manager by clicking the **Start**⇨ **Programs**⇨ **Microsoft SQL Server 2005 CTP**⇨ **Configuration Tools**⇨ **SQL Configuration Manager** menu item.

2. Navigate to the Protocols for **SQLEXPRESS** node under the **SQL Server 2005 Network Configuration** node.

3. Right-click **TCP/IP** and click **Enable** from the pop-up menu, so that you see a screen similar to the one shown in Figure 6.4. Note, if you wish to have your applications connect by using the SQL Native Client, you'll have to enable the same protocols under the **SQL Native Client Configuration** node.

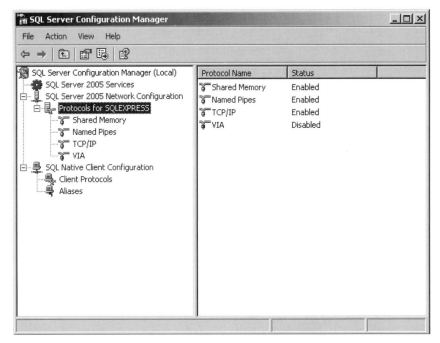

Figure 6.4: Enabling the TCP/IP Protocol.

4. Under the **Protocols for SQLEXPRESS** node, click the **TCP/IP** node. You'll likely see three entries on the right-hand part of the screen:

▶ **IP1** — Configuration for the external network adapter for remote connections. The IP address for this item is the same as the assigned TCP/IP address for the physical network card. Ensure that this item is enabled.

▶ **IP2** — Configuration for the internal loopback adapter for local connections. This loopback adapter has a special IP address of **127.0.0.1** and is used if you refer to your local computer as **localhost** or you use the .\ notation to indicate the local server. This item does not need to be enabled for remote connections.

▶ **IPAll** — TCP/IP configuration that applies to all adapters.

5. Double-click the **IPAll** item. You'll see a configuration dialog box, which is shown in Figure 6.5.

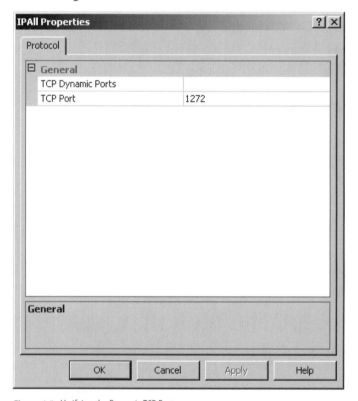

Figure 6.5: Verifying the Dynamic TCP Ports.

6.   Note the value in the **TCP Dynamic Ports** box. This is the dynamic port number used by SQL Server to help keep it secure. However, this number can change every time you restart SQL Server 2005 Express. If you want to use a specific port number every time, clear the **TCP Dynamic Ports** box and enter the desired fixed port number in the **TCP Port** box. You'll need this in Step 8.

7.   If you are using Windows XP Service Pack 2 or later, open the firewall configuration by clicking the **Start**⇨ **Settings**⇨ **Control Panel**⇨ **Windows Firewall** menu item. You may not see the menu items exactly this way, as it depends on your Windows configuration.

8.   Click the **Exceptions** tab. You'll see a list of all programs and ports that are allowed through the firewall. You need to do one of two things:

   A.   Open two individual ports in your firewall. These ports are, by default, UDP port 1434 for use by the SQL Browser service, and the TCP port you entered in the **TCP Port** box in Step 6. To do this, follow these steps:

      i.   Click the **Add Port** button.

      ii.   Enter a name that will describe the port you are opening, such as **SQLBrowser**.

      iii. Enter the port number of **1434**.

      iv.   Select the **UDP** option.

      v.   Click **OK** to save your changes.

      vi.   Repeat this process for the TCP port you entered in Step 6 and name it something like **SQLPort**, as shown in Figure 6.6.

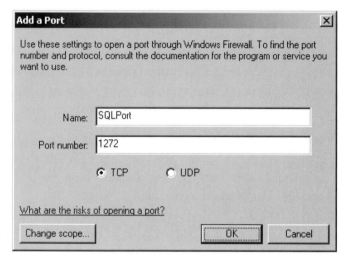

Figure 6.6: Configuring TCP Port in the Windows Firewall.

B.   Add **sqlservr.exe** as a program that is granted an exception. This lets SQL Server use dynamic ports through the firewall, regardless of the port number. Adding a program is done the same was as adding a port, except that you click the **Add Program** button and search for **sqlservr. exe**. By default it is located in **C:\Program Files\Microsoft SQL Server\MSSQL.1\MSSQL\Binn.**

9.   Launch Express Manager and connect to the remote server. If you are still having problems, see the Tech Tip box.

Tech Tip:

If you are using the April CTP or earlier version of SQL Server 2005 Express, you will likely need to change a registry value manually to allow remote connections to actually work using TCP/IP. This registry change is made on the computer that is running SQL Server 2005 Express. To make this change, open the registry editor and navigate to the **HKEY_LOCAL_MACHINE\ SOFTWARE\Microsoft\Microsoft SQL Server\90\SQL Browser** node and ensure the value of the **SsrpListener** value is set to **1** and not **0**. If you make this change, you will have to reboot your computer for the changes to take effect, as shown in Figure 4.7.

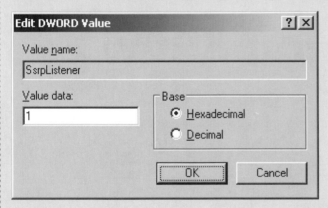

Figure 6.7: Changing the value of SsrpListener.

Summary

Because SQL Server 2005 Express is secure by default, the configurations necessary to connect to the database are not automatically enabled when you install SQL Server 2005. In fact, to enable remote connections, you have to do so in the Surface Area Configuration Manager. Enable the desired protocol, such as TCP/IP, open the required ports in your firewall, and then tools such as Express Manager can connect to the server. While it seems like overkill to have to go through such configurations, it is not because Microsoft wanted to make it difficult to administer SQL Server 2005 Express. It's simply an effort to keep your server secure and to reduce the surface area exposed to the outside world.

Did you know?

You can install multiple editions of SQL Server 2005 on the same computer. If you do, you'll see all editions listed in the configuration tools.

Chapter 7

Creating and Maintaining Databases

It goes without saying, but before you can store any data, the database must, of course, be created. The SQL Server 2005 Express engine must be able to "see" the database before you can write any queries against any tables or other objects in the database. You can either create a new database or attach a database that was created by someone else. Attaching databases is covered in the section "Attaching Databases" later in this chapter.

To create a new database, you have two options:

1. Execute the **CREATE DATABASE** Transact-SQL statement.

2. Use the New Database Wizard in Express Manager.

Creating Databases with Transact-SQL

To use SQL to create a new database, you simply issue the **CREATE DATABASE** SQL statement. While you can specify lots of different arguments with this statement, the simplest form follows this syntax:

SYNTAX

```
CREATE DATABASE <<database_name>>
```

EXAMPLE

```
CREATE DATABASE Sales
```

While this is a very simple example, it will create a database, called **Sales**, based on the parameters configured in the model database, which is located under the **System Databases** folder.

While this book doesn't go into too much depth about the Transact-SQL language (simply because of the brevity of this book), you should know that you can create databases with different parameters by specifying additional arguments with the **CREATE DATABASE** statement. For example, you can specify the size of the database and the location of the database and log files, as shown in Listing 7.1.

```
CREATE DATABASE Sales
ON (
NAME = Sales_dat,
FILENAME = 'C:\Program Files\Microsoft SQL Server\MSSQL.1\
⊃MSSQL\DATA\sales.mdf',
SIZE = 10MB,
MAXSIZE = 50MB,
FILEGROWTH = 5MB
)
LOG ON (
NAME = 'Sales_log',
FILENAME = 'C:\Program Files\Microsoft SQL Server\MSSQL.1\
⊃MSSQL\DATA\sales.ldf',
SIZE = 5MB,
MAXSIZE = 25MB,
FILEGROWTH = 5MB
)
```

Listing 7.1: Using Arguments When Creating Databases.

Listing 7.1 shows how to create the same database called **Sales** that you learned about earlier, but with an initial database size of 10 MB that can grow to a maximum of 50 MB, growing by 5 MB in each increment. Likewise, the log file is created with an initial log size of 5MB, with a maximum size of 25MB and also growing in increments of 5MB. Furthermore, the statement specifies both the logical and physical file names for the database and log. For more information about using the **CREATE DATABASE** SQL statement, consult Books Online.

Creating Databases with Express Manager

Even though issuing a **CREATE DATABASE** statement is easy, using the New Database Wizard is even easier. It prompts you for the fields that are used to create the database. To use the New Database Wizard to create a new database, follow these simple steps:

1. Open Express Manager by clicking the **Start⇨ Programs⇨ Microsoft SQL Server 2005 CTP⇨ SQL Server Express Manager** menu item. If you don't have Express Manager installed, you can download and install it according to the instructions found in Chapter 2.

2. Right-click the **Databases** node in the tree.

3. Select **New Database** from the pop-up menu. As shown in Figure 7.1, this brings up a new tab in the right-hand pane of the SQL Express Manager.

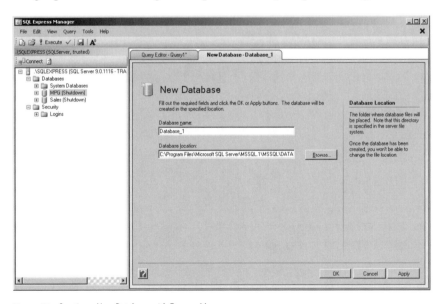

Figure 7.1: Creating a New Database with Express Manager.

4. Enter data into these fields:

    ► **Database name** — The name of the database. This name is what will appear in SQL Express Manager and will be referenced in your code.

▶ **Database location** — The folder where the database will be created. By default, the file path is **c:\Program Files\Microsoft SQL Server\ MSSQL.1\MSSQL\DATA**.

5. Click the **OK** button. The database is created in the chosen folder.

When the database is created, two files are automatically created at the same time, in the same folder:

▶ **<<database name>>.mdf** — File used to store data and database objects. For example, a database named **DB1** has data stored in a file named **DB1.mdf**.

▶ **<<database name>>_log.ldf** — File used to store the transaction log data. Likewise, the database named **DB1** has transaction logs stored in a file named DB1_log.ldf.

Attaching Databases

If you have a SQL Server database on a hard drive or file share that the SQL Server 2005 Express engine doesn't know about, you can attach it so that it becomes available to the engine. This is a likely scenario when moving databases from one server to another or when an Independent Software Vendor (ISV) distributes databases for its applications.

To attach a database, you use the **CREATE DATABASE** Transact-SQL statement, but you also specify the **FOR ATTACH** option. This statement can be executed either by using Express Manager or SQLCMD. To see how to use SQLCMD, see Chapter 2.

The **CREATE DATABASE** Transact-SQL statement follows this general syntax when you use the **FOR ATTACH** option:

SYNTAX

```
CREATE DATABASE database_name
ON PRIMARY (FILENAME='file_name')
FOR ATTACH
```

Where

▶ *database_name* is the internal name of the database as it will be referred to from your applications and from within Express Manager.

▶ *file_name* is the fully qualified path and file name of the database **mdf** file.

EXAMPLE

```
CREATE DATABASE Sales
ON PRIMARY (FILENAME='C:\Program Files\Microsoft SQL Server\MSSQL.1\
➲MSSQL\Data\Sales.mdf')
FOR ATTACH
```

In the above example, the file named Sales.mdf in the **C:\Program Files\Microsoft SQL Server\MSSQL.1\MSSQL\Data** folder is attached as a database named **Sales**.

Managing your Databases

In the April CTP version of SQL Server 2005 Express, the only two ways to manage your databases using Express Manager is to rename or delete them. You can't change any other parameters, locations, or size. If you want to change any other parameters you need to use the **ALTER DATABASE** Transact-SQL statement. Refer to Books Online to see how to use this statement, because it can get quite complex.

To use Express Manager to rename or delete your databases, follow these simple steps:

1. Open Express Manager by clicking the **Start**⇨ **Programs**⇨ **Microsoft SQL Server 2005 CTP**⇨ **SQL Server Express Manager** menu item.

2. Right-click the desired database under the Databases node in the tree.

3. Select either **Delete** or **Rename** from the pop-up menu.

Creating Objects within Databases

Once your database is created, you can then create objects used to store, manage, and manipulate your data, such as the following:

- ► **Tables** — Covered in this chapter.

- ► **Stored Procedures** — Covered in Chapter 11.

- ► **Views** — Covered in Chapter 12.

- ► **Triggers** — Covered in Chapter 13.

- ► **Indexes** — Covered in Chapter 15.

The most fundamental object to store data is the table. A table is created and stored within the database file, so, of course, the database must be created first. At the time of the April CTP version of Express Manager, you could not create tables graphically. You had to create them by using the **CREATE TABLE** Transact-SQL statement.

The **CREATE TABLE** statement follows this general syntax:

SYNTAX

```
CREATE TABLE
[database_name.[schema_name].|schema_name.]table_name
({<column_definition>|<computed_column_definition>}
[<table_constraint>] [ ,...n ])
```

Where

- ► *database_name* is the internal name of the database that will be used to contain the new table. This is optional, as the table will be created in the current database.

- ► *schema_name* is the name of the schema if you wish not to use the default **dbo** schema. It is also possible to configure a user to have a default schema other than **dbo**, by specifying this in the **CREATE USER** or **ALTER USER** Transact-SQL statements. Schemas are covered in Chapter 1.

- ► *table_name* is the name of the new table to create.

- ► *column_definition* is the definition of a column, including its name and datatype.

▶ *computed_column_definition* is the definition of a column that does not physically store data, but is computed from other columns of data.

▶ *table_constraint* is used to specify the key and index options for a table. Indexes are covered in Chapter 15.

The *column_definition* option follows this general syntax:

```
column_name <data_type>[NULL|NOT NULL]
[COLLATE collation_name][[ CONSTRAINT constraint_name ] DEFAULT constant_
⊃expression
]|[ IDENTITY [( seed ,increment )][ NOT FOR REPLICATION ]]
[ROWGUIDCOL][<column_constraint>[ ...n ]]
```

Where *data_type* can be any of the types shown in Table 7.1.

Data Type	Description	Storage Space
bigint	Numeric type that stores values in the range of -9,223,372,036,854,775,808 to 9,223,372,036,854,775,807.	8 Bytes
binary	Stores fixed-length binary data up to 8000 bytes.	Up to 8000 Bytes
bit	Numeric type that stores values of 0 or 1.	1 Byte for every 8 bit columns
char	Stores fixed-length character data.	Up to 8000 Bytes
cursor	Stores database cursors.	variable
datetime	Stores date and time values from January 1, 1753 through December 31, 9999.	8 Bytes
decimal	Numeric type that allows you to specify the precision and scale of the number to be stored.	1-9 precision: 5 Bytes10-19 precision: 9 Bytes20-28 precision: 13 Bytes29-38 precision: 17 Bytes
float	Stores floating-point numbers and lets you specify the mantissa bits value.	1-24 bits: 4 Bytes25-53 bits: 8 Bytes
image	Stores image data. This data type is used for backward compatibility with SQL Server 2000 and is replaced in SQL Server 2005 with the **varbinary(MAX)** data type.	Up to 2,147,483,647 Bytes
int	Numeric type that stores values in the range of -2,147,483,648 to 2,147,483,647.	4 Bytes

Table 7.1: Data Types Available in SQL Server 2005 Express.

Data Type	Description	Storage Space
money	Monetary type that stores values in the range of -922,337,203,685,477.5808 to 922,337,203,685,477.5807.	8 Bytes
nchar	Stores Unicode character data, up to 4000 characters.	Up to 8000 Bytes
ntext	Stores Unicode text data. This data type is used for backward compatibility with SQL Server 2000 and is replaced in SQL Server 2005 with the **nvarchar(MAX)** data type.	Up to 2,147,483,647 Bytes
numeric	See decimal.	
nvarchar	Stores Unicode variable-length character data.	Up to 8000 Bytes
real	Same as float(24).	4 Bytes
smalldatetime	Stores date and time values from January 1, 1900 through June 6, 2079.	4 Bytes
smallint	Numeric type that stores values in the range of -32,768 to 32,767.	2 Bytes
smallmoney	Monetary type that stores values in the range of -214,748.3648 to 214,748.3647.	4 Bytes
sql_variant	Stores variable types of data.	Up to 8016 Bytes
table	Stores data in a table.	variable
text	Stores text data. This data type is used for backward compatibility with SQL Server 2000 and is replaced in SQL Server 2005 with the **varchar(MAX)** data type.	Up to 2,147,483,647 Bytes
timestamp	Stores timestamp information, just as datetime.	8 Bytes
tinyint	Numeric type that stores values in the range of 0 to 255.	1 Byte
varbinary	Stores variable-length binary data.	Up to 2,147,483,647 Bytes
varchar	Stores variable-length character data.	Up to 2,147,483,647 Bytesuniqueidentifier
xml	Stores data in XML format.	variable

Table 7.1: Data Types Available in SQL Server 2005 Express (continued).

As an example, take a look at Listing 7.2. It shows a sample **CREATE TABLE** statement.

```
CREATE TABLE MPG.History.Customer
(
    CustomerID      INT CONSTRAINT pkCustomerID PRIMARY KEY IDENTITY,
    CompanyName     VARCHAR(50),
    FirstName       VARCHAR(20),
    LastName        VARCHAR(20),
    Title           VARCHAR(20),
    Address1        VARCHAR(20),
    Address2        VARCHAR(20),
    City            VARCHAR(25),
    StateProvince   VARCHAR(20),
    Postal          VARCHAR(10),
    Phone           VARCHAR(20),
    Fax             VARCHAR(20),
    EMail           VARCHAR(50)
)
```

Listing 7.2: Sample CREATE TABLE Statement.

In Listing 7.2, a new table named **Customer** is created in a schema with a name of **History** in the **MPG** database. The table contains 13 columns, most of which are not very noteworthy. The columns store customer-related information, such as the address, phone number, fax, etc. However, the first column, **CustomerID** is defined with a primary key constraint so that unique values are enforced and indexed accordingly. It also defines the **CustomerID** column as an identity field, which will automatically increment values of this field by a value of one for each new record. This is a way to effectively assign new unique **CustomerID** values for new customers. This is done only for the purposes of this example. The reality is that for a history table, you probably don't want an identity field in the table, as you need to be able to move data from your live database to history, while preserving all values.

As you can see, there are many more options for creating tables and the examples shown herein are very simple. If you need to know more detailed information about how to create table constraints (not just column constraints), foreign keys, and defaults, see Books Online.

Summary

Creating databases is very easy to do and can be done by using the **CREATE DATABASE** Transact-SQL statement or with the Express Manager application. The **CREATE DATABASE** statement can be used to create a new database or attach an existing one. Once you have the database created, you're ready to begin creating tables and other objects to store and manipulate your data. The **CREATE TABLE** statement is used to create your tables that will store data. There are many options for this statement that are not covered here, but this chapter showed you how to create a basic table with an identity column and primary key. It also showed you the basic syntax needed to create a new database, attach an existing database, and create tables to store your data.

Chapter 8

Deployment

Once you have created your SQL Server 2005 Express database and all the desired objects (tables, views, stored procedures, etc.) and configured security for those objects, you are ready to deploy it into a production environment. The following scenarios typify how SQL Server 2005 Express databases are deployed:

▶ An Independent Software Vendor (ISV) distributes a database with its application.

▶ A database for a Web site contains basic functionality such as lookup tables and basic user information. If there are many users or lots of information, SQL Server 2005 Express is probably not the correct edition of SQL Server 2005 for your Web site.

▶ Sharing databases amongst students in a classroom.

One of the design goals for the Express edition of SQL Server 2005 is to simplify the deployment of databases into the scenarios described above. While the Enterprise and Standard editions of SQL Server 2005 are likely not to be moved to another server, the Express edition is. Therefore, you have a couple of choices in how to deploy your databases to another server. This chapter outlines those choices, concepts, and the mechanics of deploying your databases.

User Instances

As part of the tight integration with Visual Studio, SQL Express includes a feature called *User Instances* that makes SQL Server act much more like a desktop database than a server database. The Visual Studio tools treat a User Instance database like a file. When you create a database, it shows up as a file in your project view and can be versioned like any other file in your project. You can distribute your database with the rest of your project by copying the **.mfd** and **.ldf** database and log files on the release media. When you distribute your application using Click Once deployment, the SQL Express files will be downloaded and installed automatically, so the application can install and run with no user intervention. See the section "Click Once" later in this chapter for more information.

In order to treat a database as a file, you must be able to attach and detach database files knowing only the database file name. SQL Server supports an ADO.NET feature to provide this attachment functionality with a connection string attribute called **AttachDBFileName**. With the **AttachDBFileName** attribute in the connection string, SQL Server will attach the file to SQL Server and return a connection to the newly attached database. Attaching a database has two limitations:

▶ SQL Server will not allow two databases to have the same name, or else name collisions will occur.

▶ You need **sysadmin** permissions to attach a database, which gives administrative privileges to every user that opens a connection to the database. This is not a practical or secure way to open a connection to a database.

SQL Express solves these problems with the User Instance feature. When you include **User Instance = true** in the connection string, a unique name is generated for the database and a new instance of the SQL Server service is started. You will learn how this property is set when you read Chapter 8. Instead of running with administrative privileges, this new instance runs with the same credentials as those of the user opening the connection.. The database file is attached to the new instance, a named pipe is created pointing to the database, then ADO.NET opens a connection to the named pipe and returns the connection to the application.

Because the database instance is running as the same Windows user as the application, the application has full administrative rights to the attached database. This means that the Visual Studio user has full rights to create whatever database object the application requires. When the application is deployed, the deployed application has full rights to the database without them being specifically granted. This is similar to the access that a file-based database gives. A user who has Windows access to the database file has full access to the data.

The key thing to remember about the concept of User Instances is that in almost all respects, each is a completely separate copy of SQL Server. Some of the implications of attaching database as user instances are:

▶ Each user instance has its own copy of **sqlservr.exe** running with the credentials of the user who opened the connection.

▶ Every user that has opened a User Instance connection has a full set of system databases in their user directory: **master**, **msdb**, **tempdb**.

▶ Each instance opens the database file with exclusive access. This means that two different users can't have the same database file open simultaneously. For example, the Visual Studio 2005 IDE and an ASP.NET Web application can't have the same database open simultaneously. Visual Studio 2005 manages the connections for you, but only if you start the Web page from within the IDE. If you open the Web page from a browser while Visual Studio 2005 has the database open, the ASP page won't be able to connect because Visual Studio has the file open. If you need to support multiple users connecting to the database simultaneously, remove the **User Instance = true** clause from the connection string. This will allow the database to be opened as a shared SQL Server database.

▶ Because the User Instance is running with the user's credentials, the user that owns the instance must have permission to read and write the file. This means that a database file that works fine when attached to the normal SQL Express instance may not work when attached as a User Instance, unless read-write permissions are granted. The opposite can also be true.

▶ To provide more security, some of the user's permissions are removed before the User Instance is started. For example, if the user starting a User Instance is a Windows administrator, the administrative permissions won't apply to the User Instance. This means that file permissions must be granted to the user specifically.

Tech Tip:

Like most software features, User Instances need an acronym. The obvious acronym would be "UI" but that one is already taken, so the User Instance feature is called "RANU," which stands for Run As Normal User. This isn't an official name, but you will often hear the User Instance feature referred to as RANU.

FREE

Bonus:

A more in-depth discussion of User Instances is available as a free bonus chapter after you register this book on the Web. See the last page in this book for more information on how to do this.

XCopy Deployment

Because using User Instances treats a SQL Server 2005 Express database just like it was a file (which it really is), you can XCopy that file along with the rest of your project to its destination. *XCopy* deployment is a legacy term that is left over from the DOS days. **XCopy** is a DOS command that copies all files in the current folder and all child folders to the desired location. In fact, you don't have to use the **XCopy** application at all to XCopy your applications. It's more the concept that your Visual Studio 2005 applications and attached Visual Studio 2005 Express databases and their connections are just copied to a target location and they just work.

To XCopy an application, follow these few steps:

1. Compile your application for release. Refer to the Visual Studio 2005 documentation for information on how to do this.

2. After your application is compiled, navigate to the **Release** folder in the folder hierarchy dictated by your project. A sample project, called **BookApp**, is shown in Figure 8.1. Notice in Figure 8.1 that there are eight files. There were all placed in the **Release** folder automatically when you compiled the application.

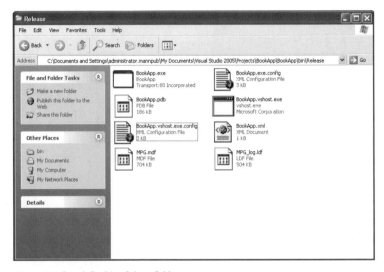

Figure 8.1: Sample BookApp Release Folder.

3.   Copy the **Release** folder in its entirety to the desired location. Provided that the same version of the .NET Framework is running on the target computer, the application will just work!

Click Once

Click Once is related to XCopy, except that you don't have to actually navigate to the folder structure and manually copy the files that make up your application. Instead, Click Once creates a setup program for other users to actually install the application. To use Click Once, follow this simple procedure:

1.   Compile your application.

2.   Click the **Build⇨Publish<Application>** menu item, where *Application* is the name of your application. This brings up the Publish Wizard shown in Figure 8.2.

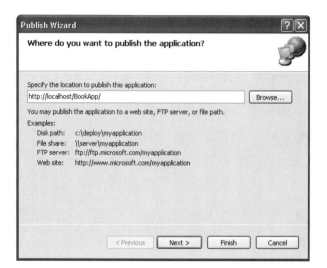

Figure 8.2: Click Once Publish Wizard.

3. Specify the location where you wish to publish the application. You can publish to a disk path, file share, FTP server, or Web site. For example, if you want to publish to the **\\SERVER01\Apps** file share, simply enter that into the box provided.

4. Click the **Next** button.

5. Select how the application will be installed by the users. You have these choices:

    ▶ From a Web site

    ▶ From a UNC path or file share

    ▶ From a CD-ROM or DVD-ROM

6. Click the **Next** button.

7. Select whether this application will be available offline.

8. Click the **Next** button.

9. Verify your publish parameters. If you want to correct anything, click the **Back** button.

10. Click the **Finish** button.

When Click Once is finished, an application setup is created automatically in the location that you specified. A Web page is generated to let your users click to install the application (even if you deployed to a file share and not a Web site). Figure 8.3 shows this Web page to let users install the application.

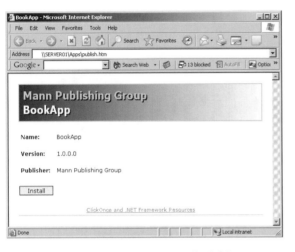

Figure 8.3: Application Setup Web Page Generated by Click Once.

Tech Tip:

If your application includes a SQL Server 2005 Express database and you use the Click Once feature, the user application setup process (when the user clicks the **Install** button) will actually download and install SQL Server 2005 Express from the Microsoft Web site to ensure that the database actually runs.

Summary

Deploying your Visual Studio 2005 and SQL Server 2005 Express applications could not be easier. If you include a SQL Server 2005 Express database in your Visual Studio 2005 projects, it automatically sets the **User Instance = true** attribute on the connection string. Once you develop your applications in Visual Studio 2005, all you need to do to deploy them is to XCopy them to a location where users will run the application, or use Click Once to automatically create a setup program for users to execute to install the application. This short chapter showed you how to do all of this.

Did you know?

The Click Once feature of Visual Studio 2005 will install all files that are included in your Visual Studio 2005 projects, even if they are not related to SQL Server 2005 or Visual Studio 2005.

Development

Chapter 9

Data Access

Data access is a term used to describe the technology for connecting to SQL Server 2005 and accessing its data. SQL Server 2005 has many improvements in the area of data access over its SQL Server 2000 predecessor. This chapter outlines the data access features and technologies of SQL Server 2005.

Note:

Data access technologies are available for use with all editions of SQL Server 2005, including the Express edition, so very little distinction is made in this chapter, with the exception of attaching a database.

MDAC

Microsoft Data Access Components (MDAC) is a set of technologies that are used to connect to a database, including SQL Server. While MDAC is supported in SQL Server 2005, if you are developing new applications for use with SQL Server 2005, it is recommended not to use MDAC, but SNAC instead. See "SNAC" later in this chapter for more information. MDAC is part of the Windows operating system and is not distributed with any edition of SQL Server 2005.

MDAC is comprised of many different technologies to allow virtually any application to connect to any kind of database—not just SQL Server. In fact, MDAC includes these components:

► **OLE DB** — Object Linking and Embedding for Databases. A Microsoft COM-based technology that provides an object model that allows applications to programmatically access data sources. Furthermore, OLE DB exposes the object model that is appropriate to the data store that is being accessed. For example, the object model for connecting to an Excel spreadsheet is not the same as the one used to connect to a SQL Server database.

► **ADO** — ActiveX Data Objects. A set of programming objects with very low overhead that provides access to the more complex OLE DB programming model. ADO is a technology that you would typically use from within a Visual Studio 6.0 environment, as it follows a familiar object paradigm that programmers can easily adopt. There are additional ADO-related technologies that let your application connect to specialized data sources, such as:

  • **ADOMD** — ActiveX Data Objects Multidimensional. A set of objects for programming Analysis Services (OLAP) multidimensional cubes.

  • **ADOX** — ActiveX Data Objects Extensions. A set of objects that use standard DDL Transact-SQL to modify database schemas. ADOX also includes object for modifying the security aspects of a database.

► **ODBC** — Open Database Connectivity. A "catch-all" technology that lets your applications connect to many different types of data sources, including AS/400, Oracle, flat files, and more. ODBC is an open standard, so any software vendor can provide drivers to its database technology and allow it to easily work with your applications.

ADO.NET

ADO.NET is a version of ADO that is part of the .NET Framework. It provides a set of programming objects that can be easily incorporated into your Visual Studio .NET applications. ADO.NET is made up of set of classes that are already built into the .NET Framework, so if you are building a .NET application, you only need to make sure that the .NET Framework is installed or deployed in the target environment. Listing 9.1 shows a simple example in Visual Basic .NET of how to use ADO.NET objects to connect to a SQL Server data source, execute a simple query, and fill a data grid with the values from the query. These objects are made available through MDAC.

```
1:         'declare local variables
2:         Dim DataSource As String
3:         Dim UserID As String
4:         Dim Password As String
5:         Dim UseDB As String
6:         Dim SQLStatement As String
7:
8:         'initialize variables
9:         DataSource = "SERVER01\SQLEXPRESS"
10:        UserID = "Guest_User"
11:        Password = "Gue$t"
12:        UseDB = "Sales"
13:        SQLStatement = "SELECT * FROM SalesHistory"
14:
15:        'create connection
16:        Dim sConn As String = "data source=" & DataSource & ";user ID=" &
           ↄUserID & ";password=" & Password & ";initial catalog=" & UseDB
17:        Dim oConn As New Data.SqlClient.SqlConnection(sConn)
18:
19:         'declare data adapter and dataset
20:        Dim oDAdapter As New SqlClient.SqlDataAdapter
21:        Dim oDataset As New DataSet
22:
23:        Try
24:            'make connection to database
25:            oConn.Open()
26:        Catch exp As Exception
27:            Throw
28:        End Try
29:
30:        'database connection is successful
31:        Try
```

```
32:          'execute SQL statement
33:          oDAdapter.SelectCommand = New SqlClient.SqlCommand(SQLStatement,
             ⊃oConn)
34:          oDAdapter.Fill(oDataset)
35:     Catch Ex As Exception
36:          Throw
37:     Finally
38:          'fill datagrid with dataset values
39:          DataGrid1.DataSource = oDataset
40:
41:          'cleanup
42:          oDAdapter.Dispose()
43:          oDAdapter = Nothing
44:          oDataset.Dispose()
45:          oDataset = Nothing
46:          oConn.Close()
47:          oConn.Dispose()
48:          oConn = Nothing
49:     End Try
```

Listing 9.1: ADO.NET Programming Example in Visual Basic .NET.

In Listing 9.1, lines 2-6 declare local variables that are used in the code. Line 9 specifies a SQL Server 2005 Express instance called **SQLExpress** on a server named **SERVER01**. Lines 10 and 11 set the user ID and password that are used to connect to the data source. Line 13 indicates the SQL statement that is to be executed in the database specified in line 12. Line 16 builds a connection string. Line 17 declares a database connection object by using the **SqlConnection** object for a **SqlClient**. However, the connection is not actually made yet.

Line 20 declares a **SqlDataAdapter** object, which is an intermediary that connects the database itself to a **DataSet** object. The **DataSet** object, which contains the actual returned data, is declared in line 21.

The code between lines 23 and 49 is used to do the majority of the "work" in retrieving the data from the database. Because there are many things that could go wrong during the process, structured exception handling is incorporated with **Try...Catch** statements.

Line 25 actually creates the connection to the database by using the connection string parameters. As long as the connection is made without error, line 33 instantiates a new **SqlDataAdapter** object based on the open connection represented by the **oConn** object and executes the SQL statement indicated in line 13. Line 34 creates a **DataSet** object from the values retrieved by the **SqlDataAdapter**. The **DataSet** object can then be used by a data grid. If any errors occur while creating the **SqlDataAdapter** or the **DataSet**, an error will be thrown in line 36. Line 39 is used to bind a data grid to the **DataSet** object that was just created to dynamically display the data from the database using the established connection. Lines 42-48 are simply used to clean up the objects and free memory.

Tech Tip:

Another option for connecting to a server instead of specifying a user ID and password is to use integrated security. This is a more secure way to access a database, whereby the currently logged on user's credentials are used to connect to a server. This way, a user ID and password are not stored in clear text for anyone to read. If you wanted to use integrated security, you would change your connection string to look like this:

```
Dim sConn As String = "data source=" & DataSource & ";Integrated
Security=SSPI;initial catalog=" & UseDB
```

SNAC

SQL Native Access Client (SNAC) is a new data provider available in SQL Server 2005 that is optimized for very fast connections to a SQL Server 2005 database, including the Express edition, while having a very low footprint. For new applications, it is recommended that SNAC be used to make connections to a SQL Server 2005 database.

SNAC is not just another in a sea of data access technologies. It is specifically designed to take advantage of some of the unique features of SQL Server 2005, like the new XML data type, user-defined types, and MARS (Multiple Active Result Sets). In essence, you can think of SNAC as the SQL Server 2005 version of OLE DB, ODBC, and ADO. You can certainly use MDAC to connect to a SQL Server 2005 Express server, but it is just as easy to make the switch to SNAC. After all, even if you are not going to take advantage of some of the new SQL Server 2005 features, you'll gain a performance advantage just by switching to SNAC.

So, why have another data access technology? The main motivation for Microsoft to create a new technology is so that data access is not part of the operating system and that SNAC can be redistributed with your application and database. Allowing redistribution in this way means that you don't have to be concerned about later versions of MDAC breaking your applications. Your clients will always have the correct version of the data access libraries.

Making the connection to a database through SNAC is not unlike the way you would for MDAC, which was shown in Listing 9.1. In fact, to use SNAC the same way as was shown in Listing 9.1, you only need to change four lines of code, as shown in Listing 9.2.

```
16:    Dim sConn As String = "Provider=SQLNCLI.1;data source=" & DataSource &
↻";user ID=" & UserID & ";password=" & Password & ";initial catalog=" & UseDB
17:    Dim oconn As New OleDb.OleDbConnection(sConn)
20:    Dim oDAdapter As New OleDb.OleDbDataAdapter
33:        oDAdapter.SelectCommand = New Data.OleDb.OleDbCommand
↻(SQLStatement, oconn)
```

Listing 9.2: Four Lines of Code that Change when Moving to SNAC.

The main issue with the difference between Listing 9.1 (using MDAC) and Listing 9.2 (using SNAC) is that Listing 9.1 uses the **SqlClient** object, which was optimized for SQL Server 2000 and Listing 9.2 uses the **OleDb** object. By using the **OleDB** object, you can specify a data provider in the connection string of line 16. This connection string contains the string **Provider=SQLNCLI.1**, which indicates to connect using the SNAC data provider. That is the main difference between using MDAC and SNAC. However, specifying a data provider is not allowed when using a **SqlClient** connection, so you must use an **OleDb** connection. Therefore, line 17 is used to define that connection. The connection itself is still made in line 25, which does not change. Because a new **OleDb** connection is established, you cannot use the **SqlDataAdapter** for a **SqlClient** object. Instead, you need to use an **OleDbDataAdapter** for an **OleDb** object, but the concept is exactly the same. Therefore, the data adapter is defined in line 20. Accordingly, the data adapter executes the SQL statement in line 33, but it must use an **OleDbCommand** for an **OleDb** object instead of a **SqlCommand** for a **SqlClient** object. It's really that simple. Of course, your application might be more complex than the samples shown here, but you can extrapolate the same concepts to determine a migration path for running your code in an optimized fashion against a SQL Server 2005 Express database.

Tech Tip:

SNAC was designed to primarily support native applications written in C++ using OLE DB, ADO, and ODBC, not for writing .NET applications.

Attaching a Database

Because of the nature of the Express edition of SQL Server 2005, it is designed to be deployed into environments that will support the data operations of an application. This application is likely to be local to a workstation, just as MSDE applications are deployed. After all, that is one of the core strengths of SQL Server 2005 Express. However, because of the nature of how SQL Server 2005 makes connections, a database must be known to an Express instance. This begs the question, "how can I deploy a database to a customer where the application does not know about this database?" The answer is that you can attach a database to an instance of SQL Server 2005 Express at runtime by indicating this with an **AttachDBFileName** attribute in the connection string.

For example, this is how you would alter the connection string shown in Listing 9.2, line 16 to use a database stored in a file named **Sales.mdf** (located in the **C:\Program Files\ Microsoft SQL Server\MSSQL.1\MSSQL\Data** folder):

```
Dim sConn As String = "Provider=SQLNCLI.1;data source=" & DataSource &
⤾";user ID=" & UserID & ";password=" & Password & ";initial catalog=" &
⤾UseDB & "C:\Program Files\Microsoft SQL Server\MSSQL.1\MSSQL\Data
⤾\Sales.mdf;User Instance=true"
```

This line of code also shows another attribute, called **User Instance**. The concept of User Instances is discussed in Chapter 8, as it mostly relates to deployment.

Summary

All editions of SQL Server 2005 include a new data access technology, called SQL Native Access Client (SNAC), which is used to expose specific features of SQL Server 2005 in ways that Microsoft Data Access Components (MDAC) cannot. Furthermore, SNAC includes additional performance improvements over its MDAC counterpart, so it is suggested that you upgrade your SQL Server 2005 applications to use SNAC.

This chapter showed how easy it is to alter code to use the new SNAC data provider to bind data to a data grid. There are many ways to write applications to use data from a SQL Server database, but this chapter outlined the basics of how to connect to SQL Server 2005 databases. It also showed you how to attach a database file to an already running instance of SQL Server 2005.

Chapter 10

Transact-SQL

Transact-SQL, also known as T-SQL, is the implementation of the SQL language that is supported by SQL Server 2005 Express. T-SQL has been supported by SQL Server from the beginning, more than ten years ago. The SQL language is governed by the American National Standards Institute (ANSI). The ANSI standard for SQL that is supported by SQL Server 2005 is SQL-99, which is the current standard for the SQL language. However, Microsoft not only supports the SQL-99 standard, but extends it even further. With SQL Server 2000, the only choice in how to create and manage database objects was to use T-SQL. Now, with the advent of SQL Server 2005, you have a choice. You can create and manage SQL Server objects by using either T-SQL or any .NET language (commonly known as Common Language Runtime, or CLR support). This chapter focuses on the T-SQL language, while other chapters in this book focus on CLR.

New Functionality

There are many new commands and features available in SQL Server 2005 Express, which are listed in Table 10.1. This chapter cannot give examples of each one, so consult Books Online to review the syntax of each command.

Command or Feature	Description
ALTER APPLICATION ROLE	Alters an application role.
ALTER ASSEMBLY	Alters a CLR assembly in a database.
ALTER CERTIFICATE	Alters a security certificate.
ALTER INDEX	Alters an index.
ALTER LOGIN	Alters the properties for a server login.
ALTER MESSAGE TYPE	Alters the properties for a Service Broker message type.
ALTER QUEUE	Changes the properties for a Service Broker queue.
ALTER REMOTE SERVICE BINDING	Changes the properties for a Service Broker remote service binding.
ALTER ROLE	Changes database role properties.
ALTER ROUTE	Changes the properties for a Service Broker route.
ALTER SCHEMA	Alters a database schema.
ALTER SERVICE	Alters a Service Broker service.
ALTER USER	Alters a user in a database.
BEGIN CONVERSATION TIMER	Starts a timer used for a Service Broker conversation.
BEGIN DIALOG	Begins a Service Broker conversation.
CREATE AGGREGATE	Creates a user-defined aggregate function.
CREATE APPLICATION ROLE	Creates an application role.
CREATE ASSEMBLY	Registers CLR assemblies in a database.
CREATE CERTIFICATE	Creates a security certificate.
CREATE CONTRACT	Creates a new Service Broker contract.
CREATE EVENT NOTIFICATION	Creates a DDL trigger event notification.
CREATE LOGIN	Creates a new login (either Windows or SQL Server).
CREATE MESSAGE TYPE	Creates a Service Broker message type.
CREATE QUEUE	Creates a Service Broker queue.
CREATE REMOTE SERVICE BINDING	Creates a Service Broker remote service binding.
CREATE ROLE	Creates a database role.
CREATE ROUTE	Creates a Service Broker route.
CREATE SCHEMA	Creates a database schema.
CREATE SERVICE	Creates a Service Broker service.
CREATE SYNONYM	Creates a synonym for a database object.

Table 10.1: New Statements and Clauses in SQL Server 2005 Express.

Command or Feature	Description
CREATE TYPE	Creates a user-defined data type.
CREATE USER	Adds a user to a database.
DBCC TRACEOFF	Disables global trace flags.
DBCC TRACEON	Enables global trace flags.
DBCC TRACESTATUS	Displays global trace flags.
DROP AGGREGATE	Removes a user-defined aggregate function.
DROP APPLICATION ROLE	Removes an application role.
DROP ASSEMBLY	Removes a CLR assembly from a database.
DROP CERTIFICATE	Removes a security certificate.
DROP CONTRACT	Removes a Service Broker contract.
DROP EVENT NOTIFICATION	Removes a DDL trigger event notification.
DROP LOGIN	Removes a login for a server.
DROP MESSAGE TYPE	Removes a Service Broker message type.
DROP QUEUE	Removes a Service Broker queue.
DROP REMOTE SERVICE BINDING	Removes a Service Broker remote service binding.
DROP ROLE	Removes a database role.
DROP ROUTE	Removes a Service Broker route.
DROP SCHEMA	Removes a database schema.
DROP SERVICE	Removes a Service Broker service.
DROP SYNONYM	Removes a synonym for a database object.
DROP TYPE	Removes a user-defined data type.
DROP USER	Removes a user from a database.
END CONVERSATION	Ends a Service Broker conversation.
EXECUTE AS	Defines security context for some commands.
GET CONVERSATION GROUP	Retrieves a Service Broker conversation group.
MOVE CONVERSATION	Moves a Service Broker conversation to another conversation group.
RECEIVE	Receives messages from a Service Broker message queue.
RESTORE REWINDONLY	Rewinds tape devices without restoring.
SEND	Sends messages to a Service Broker message queue.
TRY...CATCH	Supports structured exception handling.

Table 10.1: New Statements and Clauses in SQL Server 2005 Express (continued).

One special thing to notice in Table 10.1 is the long-awaited structured exception handling. This is introduced in SQL Server 2005 (to mimic Visual Studio's implementation of the same) with the **TRY...CATCH** statement blocks. The **TRY** block is used to test, or *try*, one or more T-SQL statements in a batch. If there are no runtime errors, everything will proceed as written and the batch ends, but it skips the statements in the **CATCH** block. On the other hand, if there is a runtime error, the program immediately executes the T-SQL statements in the **CATCH** block as soon as the error is encountered. Structured exception handling can (and should) be incorporated in virtually all of your Transact-SQL, including stored procedures, functions, stand-alone SQL queries, and more.

The **TRY...CATCH** statement blocks follow this basic syntax:

SYNTAX

```
BEGIN TRY
    {sql_statement|statement_block}
END TRY
BEGIN CATCH
    {sql_statement|statement_block}
END CATCH
```

EXAMPLE

```
BEGIN TRY
    INSERT INTO SalesDetail (CustomerID, SalesType, OrderID)
    VALUES (3, 4, 10203)
END TRY
BEGIN CATCH
    SELECT ERROR_MESSAGE() as Error
END CATCH
```

In the example, there is a simple **INSERT** statement. At runtime, if it succeeds without error, the **SELECT** statement in the **CATCH** block will not be executed. On the other hand, if there is a runtime error—like a permissions issue with executing the query— you'll see something like what is shown in Figure 10.1.

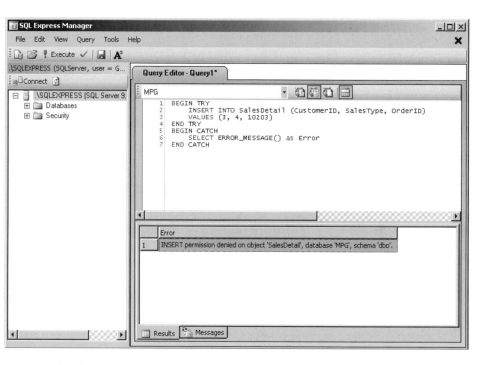

Figure 10.1: Using Structured Exception Handling.

Notice in Figure 10.1 that there is an error returned in the **Results** window at the bottom of the screen. This error is returned by the **SELECT** statement in the **CATCH** block. It returns the error by using the **ERROR_MESSAGE()** function and returning it as a column named **Error**. In fact, you can use these built-in functions in your error handling routines:

- ► **ERROR_MESSAGE()** — Returns the text of the error (see Figure 10.1).

- ► **ERROR_NUMBER()** — Returns the number corresponding to the error.

- ► **ERROR_SEVERITY()** — Returns the severity number of the error. If this number is 21 or greater, the error will not be caught with structured exception handling. Instead, the connection is terminated immediately.

- ► **ERROR_STATE()** — Returns the error state number.

▶ **XACT_STATE()** — Returns the status of whether any transactions are active.

▶ **RAISERROR()** — Generates an error back to the calling application.

Tech Tip:

The **TRY...CATCH** blocks will only work with Transact-SQL runtime errors, not syntax errors. With syntax errors, your code will not run at all, with one exception. If you run the **EXECUTE** (or **EXEC**) Transact-SQL statement and pass it a string of SQL that contains errors, the **TRY... CATCH** block will catch the error.

Enhanced Functionality

In addition to new functionality added in SQL Server 2005 Express, Microsoft also enhanced some existing Transact-SQL statements to not only provide more flexibility, but also to support new features. Some of the enhancements to statements do not necessarily affect the Express edition of SQL Server 2005, but are listed because there may be other enhancements to the same statement that does affect this edition. Table 10.2 lists the Transact-SQL enhancements made to SQL Server 2005 Express. As with Table 10.1, this chapter (and this book, for that matter) cannot cover each of these statements in detail. Refer to Books Online for specific information on any of these statements.

Command or Feature	Description
ALTER DATABASE	Adds support for database mirroring and snapshot isolation, amongst other enhanced features.
ALTER FUNCTION	Adds **Execute AS** clause for security contexts.
ALTER INDEX	Supports partitioned index rebuilding
ALTER PROCEDURE	Adds **Execute AS** clause for security contexts.
ALTER TABLE	Supports many features, such as new data types, partitioned indexes, and other new clauses.
ALTER TRIGGER	Supports modification of DDL triggers.
BACKUP	Supports mirrored data, partial backups, and more.

Table 10.2: Enhanced Statements and Clauses in SQL Server 2005 Express.

Command or Feature	Description
CHECKPOINT	Supports checkpointing at a slower rate to reduce the impact on server performance.
CREATE DATABASE	Adds support for miscellaneous features, such as snapshots and database chaining.
CREATE FUNCTION	Supports CLR user-defined functions.
CREATE INDEX	Supports partitioned indexes, XML, and more.
CREATE PROCEDURE	Supports CLR stored procedures.
CREATE TABLE	Supports partitioned tables, new data types, and new options.
CREATE TRIGGER	Supports CLR triggers and DDL triggers.
DELETE	Adds new **WITH common_table_expression** clause, **TOP** expression, and user-defined types.
DROP DATABASE	Supports dropping database snapshots.
DROP INDEX	Allows dropping and moving of clustered indexes and adds the ability to move data to other filegroups.
DROP TRIGGER	Allows removing DDL trigger.
EVENTDATA	Function that returns event information to a DDL trigger or notification.
EXECUTE	Supports pass-through commands for linked servers.
INSERT	Adds new **WITH common_table_expression** clause, **TOP** expression, and user-defined types.
OPENROWSET	Includes bulk operations for opening rowsets with **SELECT** and **INSERT** statements.
RAISERROR	Raises errors in T-SQL code.
RESTORE	Supports many restore options for databases mirrors, partial restores, and more.
RESTORE HEADERONLY	Returns new flags.
RESTORE LABELONLY	Returns new **Mirror_Count** column.
RESTORE VERIFYONLY	Supports status messages and many other restore options.
SELECT	Adds new **WITH common_table_expression** clause, **TOP** expression, and user-defined types.
UPDATE	Allows partial updates.

Table 10.2: Enhanced Statements and Clauses in SQL Server 2005 Express (continued).

Summary

Not only did Microsoft significantly expand the functionality of SQL Server 2005 (including the Express edition), but many of those features are added to the Transact-SQL language itself. Some features and statements are new to SQL Server 2005 and some are updated from SQL Server 2000.

Most of the enhancements made to SQL Server 2005 Transact-SQL are made to the statements themselves; but one notable exception is the way errors are handled. SQL Server 2005 now supports structured exception handling, so that errors can be handled gracefully and meaningfully with the **TRY...CATCH** statement blocks. This chapter showed you how to use the new structured exception handling constructs, as well as the new and updated Transact-SQL statements and functions.

Chapter 11

Stored Procedures

Stored procedures are a way to abstract the complexity of one or more SQL statements, much the way you would use a function in any programming language. For example, a stored procedure can be executed by a program that needs to return a result set of data, but does not need to understand the ins and outs of how that data is stored to retrieve the results, or even the query that is required to retrieve the data. The application simply calls the stored procedure and magically gets back the results. However, there are lots of implications involved in creating and using these stored procedures, such as the language you will use to write the stored procedure and the security that will be assigned to the stored procedure or its underlying tables.

Stored procedures have another benefit in that they are compiled and stored within SQL Server, which makes them faster to execute over running the same SQL statements directly from within your application. Therefore, it is generally a better practice to create and use stored procedures instead of executing the individual Transact-SQL statements directly from within your application.

Stored procedures are stored in the database in which they are created and can only be executed from within that same database. However, a stored procedure can access other stored procedures, tables, functions, and assemblies stored in another database, provided that the user account that is executing the stored procedure has the appropriate permissions to do so.

Tech Tip:

Before you can execute remote stored procedures, you must enable that option within SQL Server 2005 by executing these few lines of Transact-SQL code and restarting the database:

```
sp_configure 'remote access', 1
GO
RECONFIGURE
GO
```

Naming Conventions

It is a good idea for your company to have established procedures and practices for naming conventions for all your database objects. Perhaps this is even more true with stored procedures. You might want to prefix your database object names according to the type of object they are, such as **v_** for view or **sp_** for stored procedure. However, in the case of stored procedures, the **sp_** prefix can cause a problem. This is because system procedures are always prefixed with **sp_**. Therefore, you should adopt some other convention, such as **usp_** (for user-defined stored procedure). Using the **sp_** prefix can not only cause a potential issue because someone would confuse it with a system procedure, but also because there is a performance implication for using this prefix.

The performance implication exists because when a stored procedure with the prefix of **sp_** is executed, SQL Server will first try to look for the stored procedure in the **master** database. The SQL engine looking for the stored procedure in the wrong database will affect performance.

Creating Stored Procedures

Stored procedures, like most other database objects, can be created with Transact-SQL or any CLR language, such as Visual Basic 2005 or Visual C# 2005. The next few sections discuss how to create both Transact-SQL stored procedures and those created from .NET assemblies. To create either type of stored procedure, you use the **CREATE PROCEDURE** statement (although you can omit the **EDURE** part of the statement and just use **CREATE PROC**).

The **CREATE PROCEDURE** statement is used to create stored procedures that can issue SQL statements against a SQL Server, or a .NET assembly that was written in any CLR-supported language, known as a CLR stored procedure. Knowing which type of stored procedure to create, of course, depends on what you need it to do. If you need to simply get data out of the database where the stored procedure is created, it would probably make sense to create the stored procedure with SQL statements. If, on the other hand, you need to access a complex set of algorithms, it might make sense to create a CLR stored procedure, written in the .NET language of your choice. Using an assembly also gives your company the possibility of creating cross-database common libraries so developers aren't duplicating efforts in their programming. Creating these common libraries are outside the scope of this book, but it's food for thought. Read on to see how each type of stored procedure is created.

SQL Stored Procedures

Creating a stored procedure that executes SQL is as complex as you create it. It can be as simple as a single statement, or multiple branches and conditions. Listing 11.1 shows an example of the simplest type of stored procedure you can create:

```
CREATE PROCEDURE usp_CalcTotal
AS
    SELECT  SUM(Quantity * Price)
    FROM    SalesDetail
```

Listing 11.1: Very Simple Stored Procedure.

Listing 11.1 shows a simple stored procedure, named **usp_CalcTotal**, with a single **SELECT** statement that returns a sum from the **SalesDetail** table. While this statement may be somewhat functional, your needs are probably more complex. Listing 11.2 shows how you can start adding useful functionality to the stored procedure.

```
CREATE PROCEDURE usp_CalcTotalForOrder
    @OrderID    INT
AS
    SELECT  SUM(Quantity * Price)
    FROM    SalesDetail
    WHERE   OrderID = @OrderID
```

Listing 11.2: Stored Procedure Showing a Parameter.

Listing 11.2 shows basically the same stored procedure as the one shown in Listing 11.1, except that the data returned is now limited with a **WHERE** clause to a specific order ID, which is passed into the stored procedure as a parameter named **@OrderID**. Also, in order to more accurately reflect the functionality of the stored procedure, the name was changed to **usp_CalcTotalForOrder**. It is a good idea to make sure that you establish a convention for how you will name your stored procedures to not only show the basic functionality contained within the stored procedure, but perhaps also to give a clue as to what parameters it is expecting as well. This may not be applicable for all situations, as you may have many different arguments.

Note:

You'll want to include structured exception handling in your stored procedures, as discussed in Chapter 10.

CLR Stored Procedures

CLR stored procedures are written in your favorite .NET language and compiled into .NET assemblies. SQL Server then hosts the assemblies internally to make them CLR stored procedures. They are very easy to create, but there are a couple of steps that you must follow carefully before you can use an assembly inside SQL Server 2005 Express (or any edition of SQL Server 2005 for that matter):

1. Create the .NET assembly using the version of the .NET development tool that targets the correct version of the .NET Framework.

2. Install and host the assembly into the SQL catalog by using the **CREATE ASSEMBLY** statement.

3. Create a stored procedure that references the assembly by using the **CREATE PROCEDURE** statement.

Creating the .NET Assembly

To create the .NET assembly that will be hosted inside SQL Server 2005, you must use a version of Visual Studio 2005 that targets the same version of the .NET Framework as does SQL Server 2005.

You can use the .NET language of your choice to create the .NET assembly. Basically, you follow these steps:

1. Create a new Class Library project. For more information on creating projects, see Chapter 5.

2. Using a namespace, class, and sub hierarchy, write your code to perform the work that you need done. For example, take a look at Listing 11.3, which shows an example of a Visual Basic .NET routine that will calculate payments, given the number of monthly payments, the amount borrowed, and the interest rate.

```
Imports System
Imports Microsoft.SqlServer.Server
Namespace FinanceLibrary
        Public Class Amortization
                Public Shared Sub GetMonthlyPayment( _
                        ByVal NumPayments As Integer, _
                        ByVal AmountBorrowed As Decimal, _
                        ByVal AnnualRate As Decimal _
                        )

                        'declare local variables
                        Dim MonthlyRate As Decimal = (1 +
                        ⮑AnnualRate / 12)
                        Dim PaymentAmount As Decimal

                        'calculate payment
                        PaymentAmount = _
                        (AmountBorrowed * (MonthlyRate - 1)) / _
```

```
                      (1 - MonthlyRate ^ (-NumPayments))

                      'return value back to SQL Procedure
                      SqlContext.Pipe.Send(PaymentAmount)
            End Sub
        End Class
End Namespace
```

Listing 11.3: .NET Code for a Monthly Payment Calculator.

To give a context of how the code in Listing 11.3 is created, Figure 11.1 shows the code within the Visual Basic 2005 Express environment.

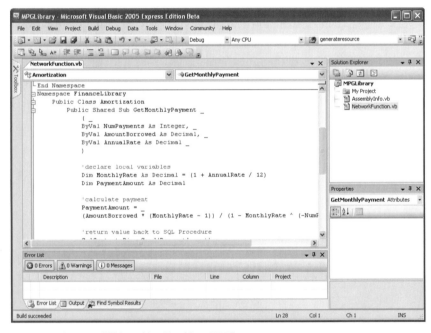

Figure 11.1: Creating a .NET Assembly in Visual Basic 2005 Express.

3. Compile your project. Make careful note of the assembly name, as you will need this to register the assembly in SQL Server. Also, make note of the location of the compiled assembly. Normally, it is located in the **bin** folder under the location of where the project code is. While it isn't obvious from the code in Listing 11.3, the assembly is called **MPGLibrary**.

There are a few specific things that you need to know about the code in Listing 11.3. Notice that all the code is defined within a namespace called **FinanceLibrary**. Then, there is a class definition called **Amortization**. Finally, the routine that does all the work is a sub called **GetMonthlyPayment**, which expects three parameters. These parameters are used in the calculation of the monthly payment.

Perhaps the most important thing to note about the code in Listing 11.3 is the line that returns a value back to the SQL Server stored procedure, which you'll learn how to define in the next section. This line of code uses the **Pipe** object of **SqlContext**, which is located in the **Microsoft.SqlServer.Server** namespace, which you import at the beginning of the code. The Send method of the **Pipe** object is used to send the value back to the calling stored procedure. That's why the **GetMonthlyPayment** routine is declared as a **sub** and not a **function**. Declaring it as a function would not return the data back to your SQL stored procedure as you might expect.

Hosting the .NET Assembly

Once you create and compile a .NET assembly, you can embed it into SQL Server so that it *hosts* the assembly. A SQL Server hosted assembly lets your SQL code have access to the procedures contained within the assembly. This is because when SQL Server 2005 hosts the assembly, it actually copies it into the database. Because the copy exists in the database, you can deploy it without fear of losing a link to the assembly, as could be the case if it was stored in a file share. In the prior section, you learned how to create .NET code with these specifications:

▶ **Assembly Name** – MPGLibrary

▶ **Namespace** – FinanceLibrary

▶ **Class** – Amortization

▶ **Method** – GetMonthlyPayment

Now that you know the individual object names involved with your assembly, you can take the steps to register it in the SQL catalog (shown in this section) and make it a stored procedure (shown in the next section). You do this with the **CREATE ASSEMBLY** Transact-SQL function, which follows this basic syntax:

```
CREATE ASSEMBLY <SQLAssyName>
FROM '<FullAssemblyPath>'
[WITH PERMISSION_SET = <Mode>]
```

Where:

- ▶ *<SQLAssyName>* is the name that will be used to reference the assembly inside SQL Server. It does not have to be the name of the original assembly.

- ▶ *<FullAssemblyPath>* is the full path of the assembly .dll file.

- ▶ *<Mode>* is either **SAFE**, **EXTERNAL_ACCESS**, or **UNSAFE**. **SAFE** is the most restrictive and means that the assembly can only access SQL Server objects. **EXTERNAL_ACCESS** allows your assembly to access network and file resources. **UNSAFE** lets your assembly do virtually anything, including access unmanaged code, so it is important to use this mode only if absolutely necessary. Only a system administrator can create an unsafe assembly. **SAFE** is the default mode if none is specified.

```
CREATE ASSEMBLY MPGLib
FROM '\\Server01\LibShare\MPGLibrary.dll'
WITH PERMISSION_SET = SAFE;
```

In the example, the compiled assembly, called **MPGLibrary.dll**, is located on a network share named **LibShare** on the server **Server01**. The assembly is referenced as the name **MPGLib** inside SQL Server, even though it has the name of **MPGLibrary** outside SQL Server.

Creating the .NET Assembly Stored Procedure

Now that your .NET assembly is compiled and hosted within SQL Server, you are ready to register one of its methods as a stored procedure. Without doing this step, you cannot actually call the stored procedure from within SQL Server. To create the stored procedure, you use the **CREATE PROCEDURE** Transact-SQL statement, just as you do if you were going to create a stored procedure that runs only Transact-SQL code. However, when dealing with .NET assemblies, you don't specify Transact-SQL statements inside your stored procedure. Instead, you indicate what .NET method to associate with your stored procedure. Here's the syntax for using **CREATE PROCEDURE** with your .NET assemblies:

SYNTAX

```
CREATE PROCEDURE <storedprocname>
    @Param1[, @Param2...]
AS
EXTERNAL NAME
<SQLAssyName>.[<ActualAssyName>.<Namespace>.<Class>].<Method>
```

Where:

- ▶ *<SQLAssyName>* is the name of the assembly that you used with the **CREATE ASSEMBLY** statement.

- ▶ *<ActualAssemblyName>* is the name of your actual assembly (without the .dll extension).

- ▶ *<Namespace>* is the namespace as you've defined it in your .NET code. Refer back to Listing 11.3 for the namespace definition.

- ▶ *<Class>* is the name of your class as defined inside the assembly. Refer back to Listing 11.3 for the class definition.

- ▶ *<Method>* is the name of your method as defined inside the assembly. Refer back to Listing 11.3 for the method definition.

EXAMPLE

```
CREATE PROCEDURE usp_GetMonthlyPmt
    @NumPayments    INT,
    @AmountBorrowed SMALLMONEY,
    @AnnualRate     SMALLMONEY
AS
EXTERNAL NAME
MPGLib.[MPGLibrary.FinanceLibrary.Amortization].GetMonthlyPayment
```

In the example above, there's a lot going on in only a few statements. That's why it was important for you to remember the individual object names that you used when you created the .NET assembly and when you registered it in SQL Server. The code creates a procedure, called **usp_GetMontlyPmt**. This will *map* to the **GetMontlyPayment** subroutine in the **MPGLibrary** assembly, but SQL Server needs to know where to locate this method. It knows based on the parameters that you specify for **EXTERNAL NAME**. The example in the prior section showed how to use **CREATE ASSEMBLY** by registering an assembly with the internal name **MPGLib**. The next part is listed as **MPGLibrary.FinanceLibrary.Amortization**, which is the actual assembly name (not the internal name), followed by the namespace, and concluded with the class name. This three-part notation must be enclosed in square brackets or quotes (double quotes, not single quotes). The last part of the external name is the actual name of the method, **GetMonthlyPayment**, as defined inside the assembly.

One more thing to note in the example is that three parameters are declared for the stored procedure. These directly coincide with the three parameters expected by the .NET, but you can change the names of the parameters if you wish.

Executing Stored Procedures

Executing a stored procedure can be done in SQL Server 2005 Express from within the Express Manager or from within your application. For more information on executing stored procedures from within a .NET application, refer to Chapter 10.

From within Express Manager, you use the Transact-SQL keyword **EXECUTE**, or simply **EXEC**, followed by the stored procedure you wish to run, and any parameters. You can either specify the parameters in the order that they are declared in the stored procedure, or specify them by name. To illustrate this point, all lines in Listing 11.4 execute the stored procedure and pass the same parameter values and produce the same results:

```
EXECUTE usp_CalcTotalForOrder 123
EXEC usp_CalcTotalForOrder 123
EXECUTE usp_CalcTotalForOrder @OrderID = 123
EXEC usp_CalcTotalForOrder @OrderID = 123
```

Listing 11.4: Executing a Stored Procedure in Express Manager.

So, how do you know if the examples shown in Listing 11.4 execute T-SQL code or .NET code in an assembly? You don't! It doesn't matter. After the stored procedure is created, you are able to execute it. That's one of the great things about SQL Server 2005. To illustrate the point, Listing 11.3 showed how to create a .NET assembly that will be hosted in SQL Server 2005. Then, you learned how to register the assembly using the **CREATE ASSEMBLY** statement and also how to create the stored procedure for the assembly using the **CREATE PROCEDURE** statement. Therefore, Figure 11.2 shows the Express Manager after executing a stored procedure created from a .NET assembly.

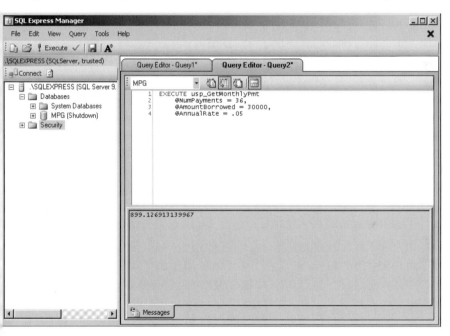

Figure 11.2: Executed Stored Procedure from a .NET Assembly in Express Manager.

Deleting Stored Procedures

When you delete a stored procedure, it is said that you *drop* it. To drop a stored procedure, you simply use the **DROP PROCEDURE** Transact-SQL command. Here's how you use it to drop a stored procedure called **usp_CalcTotalForOrder**:

```
DROP PROCEDURE usp_CalcTotalForOrder
```

Modifying Stored Procedures

Altering a stored procedure is very similar to creating a stored procedure, except that you use the **ALTER PROCEDURE** Transact-SQL command. It accepts basically the same arguments as the **CREATE PROCEDURE** command does. You might ask why you wouldn't just drop the stored procedure and create it again. The answer is that you could, but you would lose all security that you have set for the stored procedure. Therefore, you would want to modify the stored procedure instead.

As an example, refer back to the stored procedure that was created in Listing 11.2. Suppose you needed to change the datatype of the **OrderID** parameter from an **INT** to a **BIGINT**. You would do that using the Transact-SQL shown in Listing 11.5.

```
ALTER PROCEDURE usp_CalcTotalForOrder
    @OrderID    BIGINT
AS
    SELECT   SUM(Quantity * Price)
    FROM     SalesDetail
    WHERE    OrderID = @OrderID
```

Listing 11.5: Modifying an Existing Stored Procedure.

Notice in Listing 11.5 that there is very little difference in the syntax between the **CREATE PROCEDURE** and **ALTER PROCEDURE** Transact-SQL statements. The only difference is the one keyword **BIGINT**. It's really that simple to alter a stored procedure.

Security

As with all SQL Server objects, you should consider the security and permissions that you give to those objects. You want to be able to control who has permissions to execute, create, modify, and delete those objects.

In the CTP version of SQL Server 2005 Express, there is no graphical tool to manage permissions on your objects, but you can manage permissions manually. You do this using the **GRANT** Transact-SQL statement. For stored procedures, you are concerned with granting the **EXECUTE** permission on a stored procedure. Doing so lets a particular user execute a stored procedure. The **GRANT** statement follows this general syntax:

```
GRANT EXEC ON <storedproc> TO <principal>
```

Therefore to grant **EXECUTE** permissions on a stored procedure named **usp_ CalcTotalForOrder** to the user named **WebUser**, simply issue this Transact-SQL statement in the Express Manager:

```
GRANT EXECUTE ON usp_CalcTotalForOrder TO WebUser
```

System Stored Procedures

When you installed SQL Server 2005, many system stored procedures were installed as well. These system stored procedures provide a slew of functions that manage your server, populate internal tables, and allow SQL Server itself to manage its own state. While these procedures are installed for use by SQL Server internally, you can also access them if necessary. There are too many to list in this chapter (approximately 1300), so if you want to know about them, search for **sp_** in Books Online. However, there are a few that are particularly helpful that you should know about:

▶ **sp_who** – Lists the current users and processes for your SQL instance.

▶ **sp_configure** – Lists or changes a SQL Server configuration option.

▶ **sp_detach_db** – Detaches a database from the SQL Server 2005 Express engine.

▶ **sp_attach_db** – Attaches a database from the SQL Server 2005 Express engine.

▶ **sp_depends** – Lists the object dependencies for a specific database object.

▶ **sp_help** – Returns information about a database object, such as columns in a table.

► **sp_monitor** – Displays SQL Server statistics, such as number of errors and connections.

► **sp_password** – Changes a password for a SQL Server login.

► **sp_rename** – Renames a user-defined SQL Server object, such as a stored procedure or table.

► **sp_renamedb** – Renames a database.

► **sp_server_info** – Returns attribute names for SQL Server.

► **sp_stored_procedures** – Returns a list of stored procedures in a database.

► **sp_tables** – Returns a list of tables and views in a database.

To execute these stored procedures, you simply use application code or Express Manager, which is shown earlier in this chapter. The fact that these are system procedures has no effect on how you execute them. For example, Figure 11.3 shows the results of executing the **sp_configure** system stored procedure in Express Manager. Note that it is executed exactly the same way as a user-defined stored procedure shown earlier in this chapter.

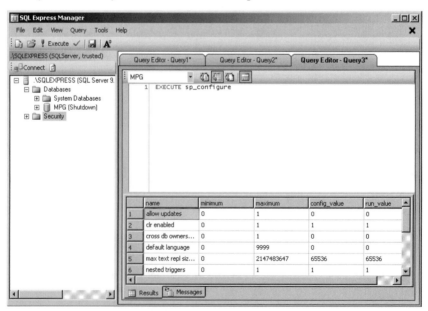

Figure 11.3: Executing the sp_configure System Stored Procedure.

Summary

There are unlimited possibilities for creating your stored procedures that execute Transact-SQL statements or even .NET assemblies that are hosted within SQL Server itself. This chapter showed you the mechanics of how to create, modify, and delete both kinds of stored procedures, but only touched the surface as to what they can do for your organization. Stored procedures can become quite complex, depending on the type of work they have to do. You should consult Books Online for more information about the options available for creating stored procedures, such as recompiling, encryption, and more.

Did you know?

A stored procedure can call another one. This is known as nesting. Stored procedures can be nested up to 32 levels deep.

Chapter 12

Views

The best way to explain a view in SQL Server is to dive right into an example. Suppose you had a table named **SalesDetail**, which stores current sales information, and another table named **SalesHistory**, which stores past sales data for any transaction that took place prior to the current month. You are developing an application that reports all sales for a given customer, regardless of which table the data is in. There are a few ways to handle this.

One way to handle this requirement is to develop a stored procedure that queries both tables and returns the data. Stored Procedures are discussed in Chapter 11. Creating a stored procedure has its advantages, but also its disadvantages. While a stored procedure can produce the desired result, you need to execute the stored procedure for it to run and subsequently return the result. Executing a stored procedure is not always possible in every circumstance. On the other hand, a view appears to your application as if it was a table. Views can be used by reporting tools, data import and export tools, and virtually any other situation where tables can be accessed. Therefore, if you ever said to yourself, "I wish I had a table to do that," you probably need to create a view instead of a stored procedure.

Sometimes views are created strictly for security purposes. You can apply separate security permissions to a view than what you have given to the underlying tables that make up the view. Therefore, you can keep the underlying tables very restrictive while giving more lenient permissions to more users. Of course, you would have to design the security so that you are not exposing sensitive data through the view when it is not necessary. For more information on security, see "View Security" later in this chapter.

Like stored procedures, views are a mechanism that you can use to hide the complexity of a query that accesses underlying tables. Views can also provide a means of securing data, because you grant permission to the view and not the underlying table that makes up the view. However, one limitation of views is that if you cannot get the result you need to create with a single Transact-SQL statement, you can't use a view. In this case, you'd have to create a stored procedure instead. After you create a view, you use it just as if it was a table.

Naming Conventions

As with stored procedures and other database objects, it is a good idea for your company to establish procedures and practices for naming conventions. It is a common convention that views are prefixed with the v_. Therefore, a view to access sales data might be called **v_Sales**, regardless of the tables it queries to retrieve the actual data.

Note:

SQL Server 2005 comes with preinstalled system views, which do not follow this naming convention.

Creating Views

Creating views is done in Transact-SQL. Views can also be created using SMO objects or a SQL Command object. To create a view, you use the **CREATE VIEW** Transact-SQL statement. It follows this general syntax:

SYNTAX

```
CREATE VIEW [schema_name.]view_name[(column[ ,...n ])]
[WITH <view_attribute>[ ,...n ]]
AS
[WITH <common_table_expression>]
<select_statement>
[WITH CHECK OPTION]
```

Where:

▶ *schema_name* is the name of your schema, which is completely optional.

▶ *view_name* is the name that you will use to refer to your object in SQL Server.

▶ *column* is a listing of the column names in your view. It is not necessary to explicitly specify column names if you want your view to expose the same column names as those from the underlying tables. However, you can specify an alias for the underlying table columns if you wish.

▶ *view_attribute* can be either **ENCRPTION**, **SCHEMABINDING**, or **VIEW_METADATA**. While this is completely optional, if you specify **ENCRYPTION**, the text of the **CREATE VIEW** statement itself will be encrypted when it is stored in SQL Server. **SCHEMABINDING** does as it suggests. It binds the view to a specific schema. **VIEW_METADATA** sends metadata about the view itself to the client, instead of the underlying tables that comprise the view. All of these optional attributes are considered to be advanced features and are not covered in this book.

▶ *common_table_expression* (also known as a CTE) is a temporary named result set. CTEs are not covered in this book.

▶ *select_statement* is the main part of the view which comprises your Transact-SQL **SELECT** statement to retrieve your data.

▶ **WITH CHECK OPTION** is used to enforce that the modification of data conforms to the **SELECT** statement, so that modified data remains visible in the view.

Before you create the actual view, it is best to make sure that the SQL statement specified by the *<select_statement>* works the way you intend it to. For example, suppose you wanted to create a simple view that selects data from a table called **SalesDetail**. Here's what such a simple **SELECT** statement would look like:

```
SELECT *
FROM SalesDetail
```

Therefore, to create a simple view called **v_Sales** that uses the above **SELECT** statement, here's what you would do:

```
CREATE VIEW v_Sales
AS
SELECT *
FROM SalesDetail
```

It's as simple as that. However, in reality, your **SELECT** statement would likely be more complex. In fact, almost anything that is valid for a traditional **SELECT** statement is valid for use in a view. You can do things like:

► Include a **WHERE** clause to filter data.

► Use a **UNION** keyword to join multiple **SELECT** statements.

► Create computed columns that are not part of the underlying tables.

► Include **INNER JOIN** and **OUTER JOIN** clauses to join multiple tables in a single **SELECT** statement.

To take a more complex example, suppose you wanted to create a view based on joining two tables together. Listing 12.1 shows how to do this:

```
CREATE VIEW v_TodaysOrders
AS

SELECT
    c.CustomerID,
    c.CompanyName,
    c.DiscountPct,
    sh.OrderID,
    sh.PONum,
    sh.TotalSale,
    sh.Timestamp
FROM Customer c
    JOIN SalesHeader sh
    ON sh.CustomerID = c.CustomerID
WHERE
    DATEPART(month, sh.Timestamp) + DATEPART(day, sh.Timestamp) +
    DATEPART(year, sh.Timestamp) = DATEPART(month, GETDATE()) +
    DATEPART(day, GETDATE()) + DATEPART(year, GETDATE())
```

Listing 12.1: A Complex View that Joins Multiple Tables.

Listing 12.1 might look a little complicated, but if you break it down into logical parts, it's really quite easy. There are two tables, **Customer** and **SalesHeader**. The **Customer** table contains customer information about the company and the **SalesHeader** table contains information about each individual order. The common link between the two tables is the **CustomerID** field, so the tables are joined on that field. Based on knowing about the two tables, some of the columns returned are from each of the two tables. However, not all data is returned by the view. Only data for the current day is returned. This happens in the **WHERE** clause. Because the **Timestamp** column in the **SalesHeader** table contains a date and time, you can't just compare it with what gets returned from the **GETDATE** function because it contains a component of time as well. Therefore, the timestamp will never equal the **GETDATE** value, so instead Listing 12.1 extracts only the date portion with the **DATEPART** function and compares that between the two values.

Partitioned Views

To take a more complex approach to using a view, suppose your database is designed in such a way that only the current month's sales data is stored in a **SalesDetail** table, while all historical sales data is stored in a **SalesHistory** table. This is a perfectly legitimate approach so that the performance of the everyday **SalesDetail** table is not degraded by the vast amount of data in the **SalesHistory** table. This is known as *partitioned data*. To return data from both tables at once, you create a view of the partitioned data, known as a *partitioned view*, which joins these two tables together using a **UNION** clause. Listing 12.2 shows how you would create such a view.

```
CREATE VIEW v_Sales
AS

SELECT *
FROM SalesDetail
WHERE SalesType = 5

UNION

SELECT *
FROM SalesHistory
WHERE SalesType = 5
```

Listing 12.2: Creating a Partitioned View with a UNION Clause.

Notice in Listing 12.2 that there are two separate **SELECT** SQL statements joined by a **UNION** clause. Each **SELECT** statement returns data from a table, but the results are combined and returned through the view. Furthermore, the view definition shown in Listing 12.2 does not return all data from the table, but only the data for a **SalesType** value that equals 5. Therefore, the view provides a mechanism to secure part of the data because it does not and can not return all data from the underlying tables with the **WHERE** clause in place.

Note:

It is not supported in the Express edition of SQL Server 2005, but if you are using any other edition, you can also create partitioned views which access data from more than one server, which are known as *Distributed Partitioned Views*.

Using Views

Once your view is created, you are ready to use it with Transact-SQL. The SQL statements that you issue against a view are the same as you would issue against a table. For example, here's how you would select all data from the view that was created in Listing 12.1:

```
SELECT * FROM v_TodaysOrders
```

Remember that this view limited the data displayed though the view to orders which were created today. However, you can further limit the data returned through the view with a **WHERE** clause. For example, if you wanted to return today's orders only for a customer with a **CustomerID** of **342**, here's how you would do that:

```
SELECT * FROM v_TodaysOrders
WHERE CustomerID = 342
```

Up to this point, you have only seen that views are used to select data. However, depending on the complexity of the view, you can also use them to insert, update, or delete data. For example, consider the view definition shown in Listing 12.3.

```
CREATE VIEW v_Customer
AS
SELECT
    CustomerID,
    CompanyName,
    DiscountPct
FROM Customer
```

Listing 12.3: Sample View for Inserting, Updating, or Deleting.

Because the view represents a single underlying table, it would be easy to write a query that inserts, updates, or deletes data. Here's an example of how to delete data through the view:

```
DELETE FROM v_Customer
WHERE CustomerID = 64
```

Notice how the **WHERE** clause is used to limit the rows that are deleted through the view, just as you would do with a table. Inserting and updating work the same way.

The difficulty arises when there are multiple underlying tables that make up the view. Depending on how the data is stored and whether it repeats through the view will dictate whether the data can be updated through the view.

Deleting Views

When you delete a view, it is said that you *drop* it. To drop a view, you simply use the **DROP VIEW** Transact-SQL command. Here's how you use it to drop a view called **v_TodaysOrders**:

```
DROP VIEW v_TodaysOrders
```

Modifying Views

Altering a view is very similar to creating a view, except that you use the **ALTER VIEW** Transact-SQL command. It accepts basically the same arguments as the **CREATE VIEW** command does. Just as with stored procedures, altering a view preserves the security privileges associated with the view, while dropping and recreating the view does not.

To see an example, refer back to the view that was created in Listing 12.1. Suppose you needed to not only limit the order to those received today, but also limit the results to a specific type of order, where the **OrderType** field is a value of **1**. You would do that using the Transact-SQL shown in Listing 12.4.

```
ALTER VIEW v_TodaysOrders
AS

SELECT
    c.CustomerID,
    c.CompanyName,
    c.DiscountPct,
    sh.OrderID,
    sh.PONum,
    sh.TotalSale,
    sh.Timestamp
FROM Customer c
    JOIN SalesHeader sh
    ON sh.CustomerID = c.CustomerID
WHERE
    OrderType = 1
    AND DATEPART(month, sh.Timestamp) + DATEPART(day, sh.Timestamp) +
    DATEPART(year, sh.Timestamp) = DATEPART(month, GETDATE()) +
    DATEPART(day, GETDATE()) + DATEPART(year, GETDATE())
```

Listing 12.4: Modifying an Existing Stored View.

Notice in Listing 12.4 that there is very little difference in the syntax between the **CREATE VIEW** and **ALTER VIEW** Transact-SQL statements. The only difference is the additional line that reads:

```
OrderType = 1
```

View Security

As with all SQL Server objects, you should consider security and permissions that you give to those objects. You want to be able to control who has permissions to execute, create, modify, and delete those objects.

In the CTP version of SQL Server 2005 Express, there is no graphical tool to manage permissions on your objects, but you can manage permissions manually. You do this using the **GRANT** Transact-SQL statement. For views, you are concerned with granting the **SELECT**, **INSERT**, **UPDATE**, or **DELETE** permissions on a view. The **GRANT** statement follows this general syntax:

GRANT *<permissions>* ON *<view>* TO *<principal>*

Therefore to grant **INSERT**, **UPDATE**, and **SELECT** permissions on a view named **v_TodaysOrders** to the user named **WebUser**, you can do that with a single SQL statement in Express Manager, like this:

GRANT INSERT,UPDATE,SELECT ON v_TodaysOrders TO WebUser

System Views

When you installed SQL Server 2005, lots of system views are automatically installed also. These views typically query the system tables and expose the result as a view. Some of the data returned in the views is quite complex, so using the system views can save you lots of time. There are too many system views to list in this chapter, but they are divided into two categories:

- ► **Catalog Views** — Contain information about SQL Server metadata.

- ► **Information Schema Views** — Contain information about tables stored within SQL Server.

- ► **Dynamic Management Views** — Contain information about the state of SQL Server itself.

For more details about each of these system views and the columns that comprise the view, you should refer to Books Online. But to give you an example of how they are used, here's how you would use the **INFORMATION_SCHEMA.TABLES** system view:

SELECT * FROM INFORMATION_SCHEMA.TABLES

Notice how this view (which is not prefaced with the suggested **v_** prefix) is used as if it was a table. That's because, as you learned from the beginning of this chapter, a view is also called a virtual table, so it is accessed just like a table. Figure 12.1 shows the results of running the above query.

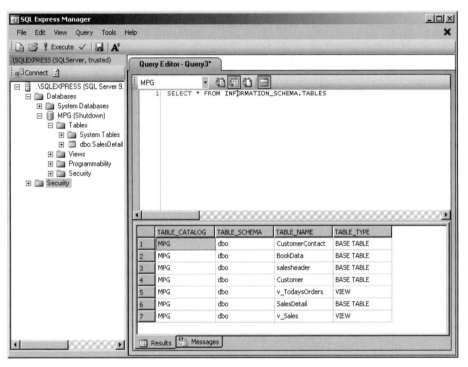

Figure 12.1: Results of Executing a Query Through a System View.

As you can see in Figure 12.1, the **INFORMATION_SCHEMA.TABLES** system view returns information about tables and user-defined views in the current database. To take the concept one step further, if you wanted to filter the data, you could include a **WHERE** clause to the usage of the **SELECT** statement for the view, as follows:

```
SELECT * FROM INFORMATION_SCHEMA.TABLES
WHERE TABLE_TYPE = 'BASE TABLE'
```

Summary

SQL Server views can be used to perform multiple functions. They can be used to query table data and return that data as a new virtual table. Querying table data can include complex queries, such as joins and unions, while hiding the complexity of those queries so the user of the view does not see it. Views can also be used to provide a level of security that the underlying table(s) of a query cannot.

Depending on how you design your view and its complexity, you can query multiple servers to create distributed partitioned views. You can even update views so that data is stored in underlying tables. By designing your views according to specific requirements, you can provide a tremendous amount of flexibility without compromising security.

Chapter 13

Triggers

A trigger is a special mechanism that executes code automatically when certain conditions are met. For example, a trigger can developed to execute when data is inserted into a table, which in turn is responsible for updating a field in another table. There are a virtually unlimited number of scenarios for using triggers. There are two types of triggers in SQL Server 2005. They are Data Manipulation Language (DML) triggers and Data Definition Language (DDL) triggers. This chapter is dedicated to showing you how to implement both types of triggers, including some of those scenarios.

Note:
DML triggers have been in SQL Server since the beginning, but they were simply known as *triggers*—without the DML distinction. However, DDL triggers are a new feature of SQL Server 2005.

For example, suppose your company has a business rule that states that for every customer in the **Customer** table who wishes to place a discount order, they must also have a record in the **CustomerDiscount** table. A DML trigger can be used to enforce this business rule.

DML triggers are used to react, or *fire*, when data or metadata changes in a SQL Server object, such as a table. Therefore, DML triggers can also be used to enforce data integrity. As a more complex example, you may want to ensure that any time data changes in the **Customer** table, your CRM system or Outlook global address book also is updated. While this type of data integrity enforcement may take a bit of programming and is not discussed in this book, it is important for you to know what data integrity is and the types of ways to extend SQL Server to ensure company-wide data integrity.

While check constraints can also be used to enforce data integrity, they are limited in what they can do. With triggers, you have much more control over the types of actions that can be taken when the trigger fires.

DML Triggers

Written using either Transact-SQL or the .NET language of your choice, DML triggers fire when data is manipulated (hence the "M" in DML). In fact, the following conditions can be specified in your DML triggers:

▶   Before data is actually inserted into a table (**INSERT** statement)

▶   Before data is actually updated in a table (**UPDATE** statement)

▶   Before data is actually deleted from a table (**DELETE** statement)

▶   After data is actually inserted into a table (**INSERT** statement)

▶   After data is actually updated in a table (**UPDATE** statement)

▶   After data is actually deleted from a table (**DELETE** statement)

There are two special temporary tables that are used in conjunction with DML triggers. They are called **inserted** and **deleted**. These temporary tables are created automatically when the trigger fires and are destroyed when the trigger has completed execution. The **inserted** table contains all the items that have been inserted into the table that caused the trigger to fire. Likewise, the deleted table does the same, but with deleted items. Updated items actually populate both tables, so you can test the original value in the **deleted** table and the new value in the **inserted** table. If you want to perform an action on the table where the trigger fired, the only way to avoid updating all rows in the table is to join the **inserted** or **deleted** temporary tables with the table that fired the trigger. This is shown in an example in Listing 13.1 later in this chapter.

DML Triggers with Transact-SQL

You create DML triggers with the **CREATE TRIGGER** Transact-SQL statement, which follows this basic syntax:

```
SYNTAX

CREATE TRIGGER [schema_name.]trigger_name
ON {table_name|view_name}
[WITH trigger_option]
{[FOR|AFTER|INSTEAD OF]}
{INSERT] [,] [UPDATE] [,] [DELETE]}
[NOT FOR REPLICATION]
AS <sql_statement>
```

Where:

▶ *schema_name* is the name of your schema, which is completely optional.

▶ *trigger_name* is the name that you will use to refer to your object in SQL Server.

▶ *table_name* is the name of the table on which you are creating the trigger, if you are not creating the trigger on a view.

▶ *view_name* is the name of the view on which you are creating the trigger, if you are not creating the trigger on a table.

▶ *trigger_option* can be either the **ENCRYPTION** keyword or an **EXECUTE AS** clause. If you specify the **ENCRYPTION** keyword, the text that makes up the trigger is not visible and it will not be replicated. The **EXECUTE** AS clause lets you specify the user account or security context that will be used when executing the trigger. All of these optional attributes are considered to be advanced features and are not covered further in this book.

▶ *sql_statement* is the Transact-SQL statement that you want to execute when the trigger fires. This SQL statement can be virtually anything (with some limitations). It can select data from one table, insert into another table, contain joins, or virtually anything else.

▶ **FOR** is used to specify that the trigger is not an **AFTER** or **INSTEAD OF** trigger.

▶ **AFTER** is used to specify that the trigger fires after the DML statement executes.

▶ **INSTEAD OF** is used to specify that the DML statement does not actually execute, but instead the trigger fires. This effectively lets you override a SQL statement.

▶ **INSERT**, **UPDATE**, **DELETE** is the keyword, or combination of keywords, that specifies the DML condition used to define the trigger. For example, if the **INSERT** keyword is specified, then the trigger will fire when data is inserted.

▶ **NOT FOR REPLICATION** is specified if the trigger should not fire if a replication is the cause of the data being manipulated.

EXAMPLE

```
CREATE TRIGGER dbo.trg_Update
ON dbo.SalesDetail
FOR UPDATE
AS
    UPDATE  SalesDetail
    SET     Timestamp = GETDATE()
    FROM    SalesDetail sd
            JOIN inserted i
            ON i.OrderID = sd.OrderID
            AND i.LineNum = sd.LineNum
```

The example shows how to create a Transact-SQL DML trigger. It assumes you have a table named **SalesDetail**, which contains a column named **Timestamp**. Any time a record in the table is updated, you want the **Timestamp** column to reflect the current time. The trigger, called **trg_Update** with a schema named **dbo**, is created **FOR UPDATE**. It fires when the **SalesDetail** table is modified with the **UPDATE** statement. What happens when the trigger fires is specified after the **AS** keyword. What happens in the example is that once the trigger fires, you want to update the **Timestamp** column. This column resides in the **SalesDetail** table—the very table that fired the trigger. Therefore, if you don't limit the **UPDATE** query in some way, every row in the **Timestamp** column will be updated. Obviously, you only want the rows affected to be updated.

To limit the rows that are affected by the action of a query, you use temporary tables that are automatically created, called **inserted** and **deleted**. These tables were described earlier in this chapter. These temporary tables are created automatically and have the exact same structure as the table that fired the trigger (specified after the **ON** keyword). To use these temporary tables, you join them by using the key fields in the table with the key fields of the table that fired the trigger (which will be the same fields). In the example, the **OrderID** and **LineNum** fields are the primary key fields in the table, so joining the inserted table with the **SalesDetail** table on these fields guarantees that the **UPDATE** statement will only take place on the values that changed. Therefore, if only one row changes in the underlying table, only one row will become updated as well.

DML Triggers with CLR

CLR triggers are written in your favorite .NET language and compiled into .NET assemblies. SQL Server then hosts the assemblies internally to make them CLR triggers. They are very easy to create, but there are a couple of steps that you must follow carefully before you can use an assembly inside SQL Server 2005 Express (or any edition of SQL Server 2005 for that matter):

1. Create the .NET assembly using the version of the .NET development tool that targets the correct version of the .NET Framework.

2. Install and host the assembly into the SQL catalog by using the **CREATE ASSEMBLY** statement.

3. Create a stored procedure that references the assembly by using the **CREATE TRIGGER** Transact-SQL statement.

Tech Tip:

The process of creating a .NET assembly in Visual Studio 2005 Express (Step 1 above) and hosting it inside SQL Server 2005 Express using the **CREATE ASSEMBLY** Transact-SQL statement (Step 2 above) is done the same way with triggers as it is with stored procedures. Therefore, each of these two operations is covered in detail in Chapter 11.

After your .NET assembly is compiled and hosted within SQL Server, you are ready to register one of its methods as a DML trigger. Without doing this step, you cannot actually call the trigger from within SQL Server. To create the trigger, you use the **CREATE TRIGGER** Transact-SQL statement, just as you would do if you were going to create a Transact-SQL DML trigger. However, when dealing with .NET assemblies, you don't specify Transact-SQL statements inside your trigger. Instead, you indicate what .NET method to associate with your trigger. Here's the syntax for using **CREATE TRIGGER** with your .NET assemblies:

SYNTAX

```
CREATE TRIGGER [schema_name.]trigger_name
ON {table_name|view_name}
[WITH trigger_option]
{[FOR AFTER|INSTEAD OF]}
{INSERT] [,] [UPDATE] [,] [DELETE]}
[NOT FOR REPLICATION]
AS
EXTERNAL NAME <SQLAssyName>.[<ActualAssyName>.<Namespace>.<Class>].<Method>
```

Where the same options are available for CLR DML triggers as they were for Transact-SQL DML triggers, except:

▶ *<SQLAssyName>* is the name of the assembly that you used with the **CREATE ASSEMBLY** statement.

▶ *<ActualAssemblyName>* is the name of your actual assembly (without the dll extension).

▶ *<Namespace>* is the namespace as you've defined it in your .NET code.

▶ *<Class>* is the name of your class as defined inside the assembly.

▶ *<Method>* is the name of your method as defined inside the assembly.

EXAMPLE

```
CREATE TRIGGER dbo.trg_UpdateSales
ON dbo.SalesDetail
FOR UPDATE
AS
EXTERNAL NAME MPGLib.[MPGLibrary.SalesLibrary.Sales].RecordSales
```

In the example above, there's a lot going on in only a few statements. Therefore, it is important for you to remember the individual object names that you used when you created the .NET assembly and when you registered it in SQL Server. The code above creates a trigger, called **trg_UpdateSales**. This will *map* to the **RecordSales** subroutine in the **MPGLibrary** assembly, but SQL Server needs to know where to locate this method. It knows based on the parameters that you specify for **EXTERNAL NAME**. The next part is listed as **MPGLibrary.SalesLibrary.Sales**, which is comprised of the actual assembly name (not the internal name), followed by the namespace, and concluded with the class name. This three-part notation must be enclosed in square brackets. The last part of the external name is the actual name of the method, **RecordSales**, as defined inside the assembly. For a refresher on how to create .NET assemblies, refer to Chapter 11, as it shows how to create them for use with stored procedures. The concept is exactly the same for triggers.

DDL Triggers

DDL triggers are used to react, or *fire*, when the structure of a table is altered. For example, you can create a DDL trigger that is used to automatically notify an administrator when a column has been added to a table. You can design your DDL triggers to roll back the DDL statement that was executed to cause the trigger to fire, so that corporate standards or security rules can be enforced. As with DML triggers, you can create them using Transact-SQL or CLR. Each is described in the following sections.

DDL Triggers with Transact-SQL

You create DDL triggers with the **CREATE TRIGGER** Transact-SQL statement, which follows this basic syntax:

SYNTAX

```
CREATE TRIGGER trigger_name
ON {ALL SERVER|DATABASE}
[WITH trigger_option]
{[FOR|AFTER]}
{EventType [..n]|EventGroup [..n]}
AS <sql_statement>
```

Where:

- ▶ *trigger_name* is the name that you will use to refer to your object in SQL Server.

- ▶ **ALL SERVER** is used to specify that the trigger fires for any database on the server.

- ▶ **DATABASE** is used to specify that the trigger fires in the database on which the trigger is created.

- ▶ *trigger_option* can be either the **ENCRYPTION** keyword or an **EXECUTE AS** clause. If you specify the **ENCRYPTION** keyword, the text that makes up the trigger is not visible and it will not be replicated. The **EXECUTE AS** clause lets you specify the user account or security context that will be used when executing the trigger. All of these optional attributes are considered to be advanced features and are not covered further in this book.

- ▶ *sql_statement* is Transact-SQL that you want to execute when the trigger fires. This SQL statement can be virtually anything. It can select data from one table, insert into another table, contain joins, or virtually anything else.

- ▶ **FOR** is used to specify that the trigger is not an **AFTER** trigger.

- ▶ **AFTER** is used to specify that the trigger fires after the DDL statement executes.

▶ *EventType* is one of the statements allowed with DDL triggers. There are more than fifty possible statements, so they are not all listed in this chapter. However, these statements include **CREATE_TABLE, ALTER_PROCEDURE**, and **DROP_ASSEMBLY**.

▶ *EventGroup* is a group of individual events that are referenced by a single name. An example of an event group is **DDL_TRIGGER_EVENTS**, which is equivalent to manually specifying the combination of **CREATE_TRIGGER, DROP_TRIGGER**, and **ALTER_TRIGGER** statements. These are all listed in Books Online and are too numerous to mention here.

EXAMPLE

```
CREATE TRIGGER trg_Audit
ON DATABASE
FOR ALTER_TRIGGER
AS
    INSERT INTO DDLAudit
        (
        DMLAction,
        ObjectName,
        UsrName,
        Timestamp
        )
    VALUES
        (
        'CREATE_TRIGGER',
        'trg_Audit',
        SYSTEM_USER,
        CURRENT_TIMESTAMP
        )
```

The above example creates a trigger, called **trg_Audit** that will fire on any table in the database when a trigger is altered, as specified with the **ALTER_TRIGGER** event type. When someone tries to modify any trigger in the database, basic audit information is inserted into a table called **DDLAudit**. To create the **DDLAudit** table, execute the following simple Transact-SQL statement:

```
CREATE TABLE DDLAudit
  (
  DMLAction    SYSNAME,
  ObjectName   SYSNAME,
  UsrName      SYSNAME,
  Timestamp    SMALLDATETIME
  )
```

This **DDLAudit** table is used to store every user who makes a change to a DDL trigger by inserting two static strings that are defined in the trigger and are inserted into the table. The trigger also uses two SQL Server functions that insert dynamic data into the audit table. These functions are **SYSTEM_USER**, which returns the current user of the system, and **CURRENT_TIMESTAMP**, which returns the current date and time from the system clock.

Tech Tip:

You can get very creative with your DDL triggers by calling the **EVENTDATA** function from within the trigger body. This function returns an XML instance that contains pertinent data about the event and parameters that caused the trigger to fire. You can use this function to create very detailed audit logs of exactly what changed in your DDL statements.

DDL Triggers with CLR

Just as with DML CLR triggers, DDL CLR triggers are written in your favorite .NET language and compiled into .NET assemblies. SQL Server then hosts the assemblies internally to make them CLR triggers. See the section "DML Triggers with CLR" for more information on how to create these triggers.

Once your .NET assembly is compiled and hosted within SQL Server, you are ready to register one of its methods as a DML trigger. Without doing this step, you cannot actually call the trigger from within SQL Server. To create the trigger, you use the **CREATE TRIGGER** Transact-SQL statement, just as you would do if you were going to create a Transact-SQL DML trigger. However, when dealing with .NET assemblies, you don't specify Transact-SQL statements inside your trigger. Instead, you indicate what .NET method to associate with your trigger. Here's the syntax for using **CREATE TRIGGER** with your .NET assemblies:

```
CREATE TRIGGER trigger_name
ON {ALL SERVER|DATABASE}
[WITH trigger_option]
{[FOR|AFTER]}
{EventType [..n]|EventGroup [..n]}
AS
EXTERNAL NAME <SQLAssyName>.[<ActualAssyName>.<Namespace>.<Class>].<Method>
```

```
CREATE TRIGGER trg_Audit
ON DATABASE
FOR ALTER_TRIGGER
AS
EXTERNAL NAME MPGLib.[MPGLibrary.AuditLibrary.Audit].RecordAudit
```

For the sake of brevity, this section does not list all possible options for use with DDL CLR triggers, as this was covered earlier in this chapter. The above example creates a trigger, called **trg_Audit** that will fire on any table in the database when a trigger is altered, as specified with the **ALTER_TRIGGER** event type. When someone tries to modify any trigger in the database, audit information is handled by the **RecordAudit** method in the **MPGLibrary** .NET assembly.

Summary

There are many enhancements to triggers in SQL Server 2005 over what was available in SQL Server 2000. Not only does SQL Server introduce the ability to create DDL triggers in version 2005, but also the ability to host CLR trigger assemblies. The creation of these assemblies is as complex as are your business requirements. However, the concept is simple. In fact, the concept is simple enough that for brevity, this chapter relies on the knowledge you gained in the stored procedures shown in Chapter 11 to create your .NET assemblies themselves. This chapter did, however, explain the concepts behind DML and DDL triggers, and illustrated when they can be used. It covered how to create them in Transact-SQL and also how to host the .NET assemblies as CLR triggers.

FREE

Bonus:

All code examples in this chapter, as well as sample .NET trigger assemblies, are available for download after you register this book (see the last page in the book).

Chapter 14

User-Defined Objects

One of the greatest strengths in programming SQL Server 2005 Express is the ability to create user-defined objects. These objects can be created with Transact-SQL and also with any .NET language and hosted as a Common Language Runtime (CLR) assembly inside SQL Server 2005 Express. This chapter covers the creation of:

▶ **User-defined functions** — Similar to stored procedures where functionality is encapsulated inside a routine, a user-defined function can be called from within Transact-SQL code that runs inline with the processing of your code. See "User-Defined Functions" later in this chapter for more information.

▶ **User-defined types** — Lets you define your own data types. See "User-Defined Types" later in this chapter for more information.

User-Defined Functions

Assuming you have permissions to do so, a stored procedure can be called from within any Transact-SQL routine, including other stored procedures. However, a stored procedure is set-based. In other words, you execute a stored procedure, it runs in its entirety, and returns to the calling statement. A function, on the other hand, runs inline with your Transact-SQL statement and is applied for every row in your statement.

Consider an example where you want to store all phone numbers without any punctuation. For example, the phone number **(603)555-1212** should be stored as **6035551212**. If you have Transact-SQL code that inserts data into a table named **Customer**, you could not call a stored procedure to format the phone number, unless you ran that stored procedure against a set of data after you inserted the data.

A user-defined function is called just like any other function that is built into SQL Server. For example, this is how you would call the **LEFT** function:

```
SELECT LEFT(CompanyName, 5)
FROM Customer
```

The **LEFT** function is built into SQL Server, but you can create your own functions and call them just the same. Here's how you would call a function that you will write in the next section, named **FORMATPHONE** to strip out all punctuation characters.

```
SELECT
    FORMATPHONE(Phone), FORMATPHONE(Fax)
FROM
    Customer
```

Creating Transact-SQL Functions

To create a Transact-SQL user-defined function, you use the **CREATE FUNCTION** Transact-SQL statement. It follows this general syntax:

SYNTAX

```
CREATE FUNCTION [schema_name.] function_name
    ([{@parameter_name [AS] [type_schema_name.] scalar_type [=default]
        }[,...n ]]
    )
RETURNS scalar_type
    [ WITH function_option [[,]...n]]
[AS]
BEGIN
    function_body
    RETURN scalar_expression
END
```

Where:

▶ *schema_name* is the name of your schema, which is completely optional.

▶ *function_name* is the name that you will use to refer to your function in SQL Server.

▶ *parameter_name* is the name of a parameter that is passed into the function.

▶ *type_schema_name* is the optional name of the schema that contains the parameter type.

▶ *scalar_type* is the scalar (single value) data type that will be used in a parameter or as the return type.

▶ *function_option* can be either the **ENCRYPTION** or **SCHEMABINDING** keywords, or an **EXECUTE AS, RETURNS NULL ON NULL INPUT**, or **CALLED ON NULL INPUT** clause. If you specify the **ENCRYPTION** keyword, the text that makes up the trigger is not visible and it will not be replicated. The **EXECUTE AS** clause lets you specify the user account or security context that will be used when executing the trigger. The **RETURNS NULL ON NULL INPUT** clause is used to indicate that the function should return a value of null if null values are specified as parameter inputs. Alternatively, can specify **CALLED ON NULL INPUT** if you want the function to execute even if null values are input. This is the default option. All of these optional attributes are considered to be advanced features and are not covered further in this book.

▶ *function_body* is the Transact-SQL that you want to execute when the function is called.

▶ *scalar_expression* is the scalar (single value) expression that will be returned from the function.

EXAMPLE

```
CREATE FUNCTION dbo.FormatPhone (@PhoneNum VARCHAR(30))
    RETURNS VARCHAR(30)
AS
BEGIN
    DECLARE @tmpPhoneNum VARCHAR(30)

    --Set initial string from input
    SET @tmpPhoneNum = @PhoneNum

    --Remove dashes
    SET @tmpPhoneNum = REPLACE(@tmpPhoneNum, '-', '')
```

```
    --Remove left parenthesis
    SET @tmpPhoneNum = REPLACE(@tmpPhoneNum, '(', '')

    --Remove right parenthesis
    SET @tmpPhoneNum = REPLACE(@tmpPhoneNum, ')', '')

    --Remove spaces
    SET @tmpPhoneNum = REPLACE(@tmpPhoneNum, ' ', '')

    RETURN (@tmpPhoneNum)
END
```

In the example above, a function called **FormatPhone** is created with a schema named **dbo**. It accepts a parameter called **@PhoneNum**, that is defined as a **VARCHAR(30)** data type and returns the same data type. Within the body of the function, several **REPLACE** functions are called that are designed to remove spaces, dashes, and parenthesis from the input string by replacing them with an empty string, thereby removing the desired character.

Creating CLR Functions

Creating CLR functions means that you create a .NET assembly in Visual Studio 2005 and import it into SQL Server 2005 Express, where it is hosted and made available for use within SQL Server 2005. In the sections below, you'll learn how to code a function and then create a function inside SQL Server 2005 Express based on the .NET assembly that you compile.

Coding the CLR Function

The same function example shown in the section "Creating Transact-SQL Functions" is shown in Listing 14.1 as Visual Basic .NET code.

```
Imports Microsoft.SqlServer.Server
Namespace FunctionLibrary
    Public Class StringFunctions
        <SqlFunction()> Public Shared Function FormatPhone(ByVal PhoneNum
➲As String) As String
```

```
        'Remove dashes
        PhoneNum = Replace(PhoneNum, "-", "")


        'Remove left parenthesis
        PhoneNum = Replace(PhoneNum, "(", "")


        'Remove right parenthesis
        PhoneNum = Replace(PhoneNum, ")", "")


        'Remove spaces
        PhoneNum = Replace(PhoneNum, " ", "")


        'return value back to SQL Function
        Return PhoneNum
      End Function
    End Class
End Namespace
```

Listing 14.1: Visual Basic .NET Code for SQL Server 2005 Function.

The code in listing 14.1 is just as simple as its Transact-SQL example counterpart. It removes dashes, parenthesis, and spaces from an input string. It does this by declaring a function called **FormatPhone** in a class named **StringFunctions** and declared in a namespace called **FunctionLibrary**. One more thing to notice in Listing 14.1 is the <**SqlFunction**> attribute to flag the .NET function as being used for a SQL function.

You compile this code into a .NET assembly which you can use to create a function inside SQL Server 2005 Express, as discussed in the next section.

Declaring the CLR Function

To declare the CLR function from a CLR assembly, you first must register the assembly in the database. This is done with the **CREATE ASSEMBLY** Transact-SQL statement. Because the **CREATE ASSEMBLY** statement is used the same way for user-defined functions as it is for stored procedures, see how to use it in Chapter 11.

You use the **CREATE FUNCTION** Transact-SQL statement for CLR functions just as you did for a Transact-SQL function. However, the arguments are slightly different. The **CREATE FUNCTION** statement follows this general syntax:

```
CREATE FUNCTION [schema_name.] function_name
    ([{@parameter_name [AS] [type_schema_name.] scalar_type [=default]
        }[,...n ]]
    )
RETURNS scalar_type
    [ WITH function_option [[,]...n]]
AS
EXTERNAL NAME <SQLAssyName>.[<ActualAssyName>.<Namespace>.<Class>].
↻<Function>
```

Where:

- ▶ *schema_name* is the name of your schema, which is completely optional.

- ▶ *function_name* is the name that you will use to refer to your function in SQL Server.

- ▶ *parameter_name* is the name of a parameter that is passed into the function.

- ▶ *type_schema_name* is the optional name of the schema that contains the parameter type.

- ▶ *scalar_type* is the scalar (single value) data type that will be used in a parameter or as the return type.

- ▶ *function_option* can be either the **EXECUTE AS, RETURNS NULL ON NULL INPUT,** or **CALLED ON NULL INPUT** clause. The **EXECUTE AS** clause lets you specify the user account or security context that will be used when executing the trigger. The **RETURNS NULL ON NULL INPUT** clause is used to indicate that the function should return a value of null if null values are specified as parameter inputs. Alternatively, can specify **CALLED ON NULL INPUT** if you want the function to execute even if null values are input. This is the default option. All of these optional attributes are considered to be advanced features and are not covered further in this book.

- ▶ *function_body* is the Transact-SQL that you want to execute when the function is called.

▶ *scalar_expression* is the scalar (single value) expression that will be returned from the function.

▶ *<SQLAssyName>* is the name of the assembly that you used with the **CREATE ASSEMBLY** statement.

▶ **<ActualAssemblyName>** is the name of your actual assembly (without the dll extension).

▶ *<Class>* is the name of your class as defined inside the assembly.

▶ *<Function>* is the name of your function as defined inside the assembly.

EXAMPLE

```
CREATE FUNCTION dbo.FormatPhone(@PhoneNum NVARCHAR(30))
    RETURNS NVARCHAR(30)
AS
EXTERNAL NAME MPGLib.[MPGLibrary.FunctionLibrary.StringFunctions].FormatPhone
```

The above example creates a function with the same name and arguments as the one you saw with Transact-SQL earlier in this chapter. However, the function is located in the **FormatPhone** function in the .NET assembly, located in the **StringFunctions** class in the **MPGLibrary** namespace in the **MPGLib** assembly.

 *Caution:*

> Strings are passed from .NET assemblies to SQL Server as Unicode strings, so you'll have to declare them with the "N" versions of the data type or your **CREATE FUNCTION** statement will fail.

Calling User-Defined Functions

To call a user-defined function, you execute Transact-SQL statements as if it was a system function built into SQL Server 2005 Express. The only difference is that you specify the schema name when calling the function. Here's how you call the function created in the prior section:

```
SELECT dbo.FormatPhone('(603) 555-1212')
```

User-Defined Types

You might wonder why in the world you would need a user-defined data type. After all, the built-in SQL Server types give you all types of numbers, including integers, decimals, currency, and more. You also get all forms of characters and strings. The answer is very simple if you consider how often you are using the same data types over and over. For example, if you constantly are looking at a stored procedure or table definition to find out how many characters you allow for an address, you'll benefit from a user-defined type. You can predetermine that every address field in your database will allow up to thirty characters, so you can define an **udt_Address** user-defined type and equate it to the **VARCHAR(30)** system type. User-defined types are often referred to as *UDTs*.

Creating Transact-SQL UDTs

User-defined types (UDTs) are created in Transact-SQL with the **CREATE TYPE** Transact-SQL statement. It follows this basic syntax:

SYNTAX

```
CREATE TYPE [schema_name.]type_name
FROM base_type [modifier] NULL|NOT NULL
```

Where:

▶ *schema_name* is the name of your schema, which is completely optional.

▶ *type_name* is the name that you will use to refer to your type in SQL Server.

▶ *base_type* is the system data type that you will use as the basis for your new data type.

▶ *modifier* is the optional specification for the base type. For example, a numeric data type can have a precision and scale specified.

▶ **NULL** indicates that the new UDT does not have to have a value.

▶ **NOT NULL** indicates that the new UDT must have a value.

EXAMPLE

```
CREATE TYPE udt_Address
FROM VARCHAR(30) NULL
```

FREE *Bonus:*

Creating CLR UDTs and their close cousin, user-defined aggregates, are more of an advanced feature and cannot be covered on these few pages. However, these are important topics. Therefore, you can download a bonus online chapter on these advanced topics after you register this book (see the last page in the book for more information).

Using UDTs

Using a UDT is as simple as using a system data type. For example, Listing 14.2 shows how to create a **Customer** table using the newly created **Address** UDT for the address-related fields. You can take this example further and define other UDTs for phone numbers, names, and more.

```
CREATE TABLE Customer

    CustomerID  INT,
    CompanyName VARCHAR(50),
    PersonName  VARCHAR(50),
    Address1    udt_Address,
    Address2    udt_Address,
    City        VARCHAR(30),
    StateProv   VARCHAR(10),
    CountryCode CHAR(2),
    Postal      VARCHAR(15),
    Phone       VARCHAR(30),
    Fax         VARCHAR(30),
    EMail       VARCHAR(30)
```

Listing 14.2: Using a User-Defined Type to Create a Table.

Summary

SQL Server 2005 Express gives you tremendous flexibility by allowing you to create your own functions and types. You have further choices in that you can create both of these user-defined objects in either Transact-SQL or by using a .NET assembly and having it hosted in the database. This chapter showed you examples of how to create user-defined functions and user-defined types. Because CLR user-defined types can get quite complex, they are not covered in this chapter, but are discussed in an online bonus chapter. If you need more detailed information about how you can expand on the functionality shown in this chapter, refer to Books Online.

Chapter 15

Indexes

Indexes are a database mechanism to query large amounts of data very quickly. This mechanism is implemented in a special structure called a B-Tree, which has been proven over the course of decades to be very efficient for quick access. You can think of a database index just like the index of a book (assuming you are not looking at a Rational Guide, as they don't contain indexes).

There are two main types of indexes:

▶ **Clustered** — An index that defines the order that rows appear in a table. Clustered indexes are typically used on the fields in a table that contain the primary key. *Primary key* fields are those that uniquely define a row of data in a table. For example, in a customer table, you will likely have a customer identifier be the primary key field because it would uniquely identify a row of data representing the customer. There can be only one clustered index on a table because data can physically be ordered only one way.

▶ **Non-clustered** — An index that is not stored with the key values in order, but has internal pointers to where the data resides. Non-clustered indexes are typically used on columns that are accessed frequently, but are not part of the primary key. You determine which columns comprise the non-clustered index based on how the data will be accessed. For example, a customer table that might have a clustered index on the **CustomerID** field may also benefit from a non-clustered index on the **PhoneNum** field, if you plan to lookup customer records based on the phone number. There can be a maximum of 249 non-clustered indexes on a table.

To understand better how B-Tree indexes work, take a look at Figure 15.1.

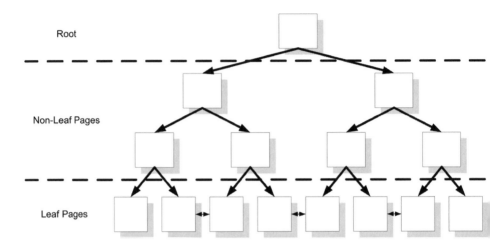

Figure 15.1: B-Tree Index Structure.

In Figure 15.1, you see three separate levels. At the top is the root, where the searching starts. In the middle are one or more levels of non-leaf pages, which simply means that they are not the end. If you think of a tree, the leaf is at the end of a branch. Perhaps non-leaf pages should be called branch pages . At the bottom, of course, are leaf pages.

The data itself is stored at the leaf-level, while the indexes to get to the data are stored in the non-leaf pages. The leaf pages are linked together from one page to the next, so SQL Server knows how to retrieve all of the data efficiently. In the case of a clustered index, the data is physically stored in the same order as the index, so the index is not stored at the non-leaf pages. It is stored at the leaf level, along with the data. In the case of a non-clustered index, the non-leaf pages are constructed and filled with pointers to the data in the leaf pages, based on SQL Server's B-Tree algorithms.

While this is easy to understand conceptually, the concept of an index becomes more difficult when the concept of updating is discussed. If you recall that clustered indexes are physically stored in the same order as the data, when you update values for the fields in a clustered index, SQL Server has to physically reorder the leaf pages, which can take time. In a non-clustered index, the non-leaf pages need to be reordered. However, this is just updating pointers to the data. Therefore, table updates on fields that participate in a non-clustered index can be faster than table updates on fields that participate in a clustered index. Indexes need to be rebuilt over time because they become fragmented, just the way a hard disk becomes fragmented.

To reduce fragmentation, the concept of a *fillfactor* was introduced. Fillfactor is a setting that you can optionally specify when creating an index that indicates what percentage of the page (either leaf or non-leaf) is to be filled. For example, a fillfactor of 50 means that each page will be approximately 50% filled before a new page is created when the index is created. Having a lower fillfactor leaves more room on each page for updates, but takes more hard disk space because more pages are created and can be less efficient for searches. However, a higher fillfactor takes less space on the hard disk but doesn't easily allow for updates. A higher fillfactor can also perform better for searching than a lower fillfactor.

Constraints

A close cousin to indexes is the concept of a *constraint*. While an index refers to a separate B-Tree structure that helps speed queries, a constraint is used to enforce business rules. Some types of constraints go hand-in-hand with indexes. This is especially true for clustered indexes. A clustered index is usually (but not always) created on primary key columns in a table. The enforcing of primary keys is technically done with a primary key constraint rather than an index, but an index can also be created on the primary key columns to speed up the very same columns. In fact, these types of constraints are available in SQL Server 2005:

▶ **Primary Key** — Enforces the primary key of a table.

▶ **Foreign Key** — Enforces referential integrity columns of a table with another table.

▶ **Unique** — Enforces uniqueness of values in one or more columns in a table, but is not part of the primary key.

▶ **Check** — Enforces that a value in a table conforms to a rule, such as the number is between **1** and **10**.

Constraints are specified as column constraints or table constraints. Refer to the examples presented in the rest of this chapter for more information on constraints. You can also refer to Books Online for more information about creating constraints with tables.

Naming Conventions

It is a good idea for your company to have established procedures and practices for naming conventions for all your database objects. This is true for your indexes as well. Just as you should implement naming conventions for stored procedures (using **usp_** or views as **v_**), your indexes and corresponding constraints that may be created automatically should follow this naming convention:

- ▶ **Primary Keys** — Prefaced with **PK_**.

- ▶ **Foreign Key** — Prefaced with **FK_** (sometimes called Alternative Keys).

- ▶ **Non-clustered, non-unique** — Prefaced with **IX_**.

- ▶ **Primary XML index** — Prefaced with **PXML_**.

- ▶ **Secondary XML index** — Prefaced with **IXML_**.

Creating Indexes

There are two basic ways to create indexes. One way is by specifying the index parameters when you create the table using the **CREATE TABLE** Transact-SQL statement. The other way is by using the **CREATE INDEX** Transact-SQL statement. Indexes can be created on two types of data columns:

- ▶ **Relational Columns** — Columns that contain relational data, such as those specified with **INT, BIGINT, DATETIME**, and more.

- ▶ **XML Columns** — Columns that contain XML data and are specified with the **XML** data type.

Relational Columns

Indexes can be created on columns in your tables that contain relational data (as opposed to XML data, which contains its own structure). You can specify relational indexes when you create the table or on existing tables. Each is described in the next two sections.

Creating Relational Indexes When Creating a Table

There are many options for using the **CREATE TABLE** statement. One of them is to specify a primary key constraint and clustered index on a single column or multiple columns. Listing 15.1 shows an example of how you can create a clustered index on a single column.

```
CREATE TABLE Customer
(
    CustomerID   INT PRIMARY KEY CLUSTERED,
    CompanyName VARCHAR(50),
    PersonName  VARCHAR(50),
    Address1    VARCHAR(30),
    Address2    VARCHAR(30),
    City        VARCHAR(30),
    StateProv   VARCHAR(10),
    CountryCode CHAR(2),
    Postal      VARCHAR(15),
    Phone       VARCHAR(30),
    Fax         VARCHAR(30),
    EMail       VARCHAR(30))
```

Listing 15.1: Creating a Clustered Index on One Column.

Notice in Listing 15.1 that the **PRIMARY KEY** keywords are specified as well as the **CLUSTERED** keyword. The **PRIMARY KEY** keywords indicate that the **CustomerID** field should be denoted as the primary key of the table, while the **CLUSTERED** keyword creates a clustered index on the column. It is a very common scenario that the primary key columns are also the clustered index columns. If you want to use the **CREATE TABLE** statement to create a clustered index on multiple columns, you would do that with a table constraint, as in Listing 15.2.

```
CREATE TABLE CustomerContact
(
    CustomerID  INT,
    ContactID   INT,
    PersonName  VARCHAR(50),
    Address1    VARCHAR(30),
    Address2    VARCHAR(30),
```

```
City        VARCHAR(30),
StateProv   VARCHAR(10),
CountryCode CHAR(2),
Postal      VARCHAR(15),
Phone       VARCHAR(30),
Fax         VARCHAR(30),
EMail       VARCHAR(30)
CONSTRAINT [PK_CustomerContact]
PRIMARY KEY CLUSTERED ([CustomerID], [ContactID]))
```

Listing 15.2: Creating a Clustered Index on Multiple Columns.

Listing 15.2 shows that the **PRIMARY KEY** and **CLUSTERED** keywords are not specified after the column names if you are specifying more than one column. Instead, they are specified as a table **CONSTRAINT** clause after the column definitions. Listing 15.2 creates a primary key constraint named **PK_CustomerContact** on the **CustomerID** and **ContactID** columns.

You can also create non-clustered indexes on tables when you create them, but only if you want to create a unique constraint at the same time. Listing 15.3 takes the example in Listing 15.1 one step further by creating a unique constraint and non-clustered index on the **Postal** column.

```
CREATE TABLE Customer
(
    CustomerID  INT PRIMARY KEY CLUSTERED,
    CompanyName VARCHAR(50),
    PersonName  VARCHAR(50),
    Address1    VARCHAR(30),
    Address2    VARCHAR(30),
    City        VARCHAR(30),
    StateProv   VARCHAR(10),
    CountryCode CHAR(2),
    Postal      VARCHAR(15) CONSTRAINT IX_Postal UNIQUE NONCLUSTERED,
    Phone       VARCHAR(30),
```

```
Fax          VARCHAR(30),
EMail        VARCHAR(30))
```

Listing 15.3: Creating a Clustered Index and a Non-Clustered Index.

Creating Relational Indexes on Existing Tables or Views

Creating indexes on relational tables when the table or view already exists is done with the CREATE INDEX Transact-SQL statement. It follows this basic syntax:

SYNTAX

```
CREATE [UNIQUE][CLUSTERED|NONCLUSTERED] INDEX index_name
    ON object (column [ASC|DESC] [,...n])
    [INCLUDE (column_name [,...n])]
    [WITH (index_option [,...n])]
```

Where:

- ▶ **UNIQUE** creates a unique constraint and index.

- ▶ **CLUSTERED** creates a clustered index.

- ▶ **NONCLUSTERED** creates a non-clustered index.

- ▶ *index_name* is the name of your relational index. Remember to prefix the index with the appropriate naming conventions that your company uses.

- ▶ *object* is the name of the object on which you will create the index. This would be the name of a table or view.

- ▶ *column* is the name of the columns in the table or view to include in the index. Each must be separated by a comma. The total size of the column names that you specify cannot exceed 900 bytes.

- ▶ **ASC** the index in ascending order. This is the default option.

- ▶ **DESC** creates the index in descending order.

- ▶ **INCLUDE** lets you specify one or more column names that are to be included in the index, but are not part of a non-clustered index.

▶ **WITH** *index_option* is one of the following options:

- **PAD_INDEX** = { **ON** | **OFF** } — Pads the non-leaf pages if fillfactor is supplied.

- **FILLFACTOR** = **fillfactor_value** — Uses the fillfactor percentage specified.

- **SORT_IN_TEMPDB** = { **ON** | **OFF** } — Sorts the index in the **tempdb** database.

- **IGNORE_DUP_KEY** = { **ON** | **OFF** } — Indicates that duplicate keys that already exist in a unique index are ignored.

- **STATISTICS_NORECOMPUTE** = { **ON** | **OFF** } — Indicates that statistics for the index are not updated. See the section "Updating Indexes" later in this chapter.

- **DROP_EXISTING** = { **ON** | **OFF** } — Specifies that the existing index should be dropped and recreated.

- **ALLOW_ROW_LOCKS** = { **ON** | **OFF** } — Specifies if the index should be created while allowing row locks on the table or index.

- **ALLOW_PAGE_LOCKS** = { **ON** | **OFF** } — Specifies if the index should be created while allowing page locks on the table or index.

EXAMPLE

```
CREATE NONCLUSTERED INDEX IX_PostalON Customer (Postal)WITH FILLFACTOR = 80
```

The example above simply creates a non-clustered index on the **Postal** column in the **Customer** table. The index is named **IX_Postal** and has a **fillfactor** of 80%.

XML Columns

Indexes on XML columns are not created during the table creation process. Therefore, you specify the creation of an XML index with the **CREATE INDEX** Transact-SQL statement, which follows this general syntax:

```
CREATE [PRIMARY] XML INDEX index_name
    ON object (column)
    [USING XML INDEX xml_index_name
        [FOR {VALUE|PATH}]
    [WITH (index_option [,...n ])]
```

Where:

▶ **PRIMARY** creates an XML index from the table's cluster key values.

▶ *index_name* is the name of your XML index. Remember to prefix the index with the appropriate naming conventions that your company uses.

▶ *object* is the name of the object on which you will create the index. This would be the name of a table or view.

▶ *column* is the name of the XML column on which you will create the index.

▶ **USING XML INDEX** indicates the name of the primary index if you are creating a secondary index. Secondary indexes are not covered in this book.

▶ **FOR VALUE or FOR PATH** indicates additional options for creating secondary indexes, which are not covered in this book.

▶ **WITH** *index_option* is the same as it was under "Creating Relational Indexes on Existing Tables or Views," except **IGNORE_DUP_KEY** and **ONLINE**.

```
CREATE PRIMARY XML INDEX PXML_OnixON Book (ONIXData)
```

The above example creates a primary XML index on the **ONIXData** XML column in the **Book** table named **PXML_Onix**.

Updating Indexes

When SQL Server queries an index to find out how to efficiently access data, it looks at parameters and a sampling of the values of the data that comprises the index. This sampling is known as *statistics*. Statistics are automatically updated, provided that you don't specify the **STATISTICS_NORECOMPUTE** option when you create the index.

There are two ways to update an index in SQL Server 2005 Express:

▶ Create a new index using the CREATE INDEX statement with the **DROP_ EXISTING** = **On** clause.

▶ Modify the index using the **ALTER INDEX** statement with the **REBUILD** clause.

This single statement shows the very simple form of how to rebuild an index:

```
ALTER INDEX PXML_Onix ON Customer REBUILD
```

For more information about rebuilding indexes, see **ALTER INDEX** in Books Online.

Summary

Indexes and their creation can become quite complex. It's not the creation of the index itself that is complex—it's knowing where to place the indexes for optimal performance, which requires a thorough understanding of how your application and database will be used. This chapter does not go into the performance tuning of your databases, but it covered the mechanics of how to create indexes on relational columns and XML columns.

Advanced Concepts

Chapter 16

Security

One of the most important things you can do in the IT field is implement security. Security issues should not be considered lightly. In fact, these issues should be planned very well. However, the first step in planning is to understand what is possible and what security features are available in your software products. SQL Server 2005 Express is no exception.

The security mechanisms in SQL Server 2005 are very robust, but the Express edition has some special features, which are discussed throughout this chapter. The reason that the Express edition of SQL Server 2005 needs a slightly different security model is because it's the only edition that is intended to be redistributed with applications. To understand the scenarios under which SQL Server 2005 Express could be used and distributed, see Chapter 1.

Before the in-depth discussion of SQL Server security begins, take a look at Figure 16.1. It shows the security model, based on all the possible security flows that can be employed using SQL Server 2005. Keep Figure 16.1 handy, as it is referenced throughout this chapter.

Security is a very complex topic and cannot be completely covered in single chapter. It could be covered in its own book. However, this chapter focuses on object-level security, including logins and roles. Network security is covered in Chapter 6.

Note:
The Transact-SQL statements shown in this chapter give you the basics and most common scenarios in using the statement. However, in some cases, there are additional options that can be specified, so refer to Books Online for a detailed look at all possible arguments and options for these statements.

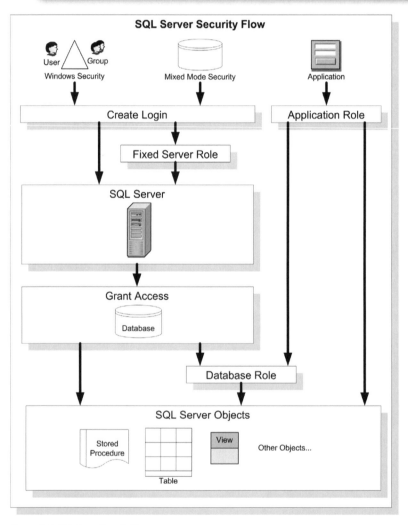

Figure 16.1: SQL Server Security Flows.

The most fundamental security mechanism is the authentication mode. SQL Server 2005 (all editions) allows two separate authentication modes that are selected during the installation process:

▶ **Windows Authentication Mode** — Also known as *integrated security*, lets you use Windows security instead of defining users in SQL Server.

▶ **Mixed Mode** — Enables you to define security users and groups that are stored within SQL Server itself or users defined with Windows security. If you are developing SQL Server 2005 Express applications that will be distributed outside your organization, it is likely that you will want this authentication mode.

In addition to these authentication modes, which are specified during installation of SQL Server 2005, you can also create application roles, which allow an application, instead of a user, to login to SQL Server. You'll read more about this throughout the chapter. For more information about installing SQL Server 2005 Express, see Chapter 2. The rest of this chapter is dedicated to outlining the security features of SQL Server 2005 Express.

Note:

Because SQL Server 2005 Express is in its Beta Preview form, there are very few graphical (GUI) screens available to administer security. Therefore, almost all security-related features have to be implemented using Transact-SQL. However, this is expected to change by the time the product is released.

Logins

Before users can access SQL Server, they must have a login that is granted access to SQL Server. Furthermore, before they can access a specific database within SQL Server, they must be granted access to that database, which is shown in the "Granting Database Access" section later in this chapter. There are two types of logins available in SQL Server 2005, depending on the authentication mode that you selected when you installed SQL Server:

▶ **SQL Server Login** — User whose credentials are stored within SQL Server. SQL logins can be used if you configured SQL Server during installation to use either the Mixed or Windows authentication modes. It is likely that if a SQL Server 2005 Express database is to be distributed outside your domain, you will be using SQL Server logins or application roles. For more information about application roles, see "Application Roles" later in this chapter.

▶ **Windows Login** — User whose credentials are stored within a Windows domain. Windows logins can only be used if you configured SQL Server during installation to use the Windows authentication mode.

SQL Server Logins

To create a SQL Server login (assuming you didn't configure SQL Server to use the Windows authentication mode), you use the **CREATE LOGIN** Transact-SQL statement, which follows this general syntax:

SYNTAX

```
CREATE LOGIN login_name WITH PASSWORD='password'
```

Where:

▶ *login_name* is the name that the user or application will use to connect to SQL Server

▶ *password* is the password that the login will use to connect to SQL Server

EXAMPLE

```
CREATE LOGIN WebUser WITH PASSWORD='WebPW@42$5'
```

In the example, a SQL Server login named **WebUser** is created with a password of **WebPW@42$5**.

Windows Logins

Just because someone has a valid login within a Windows domain doesn't mean that they have access to a SQL Server, so you have to give a Windows user explicit permissions to access a SQL Server. With respect to SQL Server 2005, you don't actually *create* a Windows login because a user who has an account in a domain or a local Windows login already had a Windows account created. However, to SQL Server, this user does not exist. You have to grant the user privilege to connect to SQL Server 2005 Express. You do that with the **CREATE LOGIN** Transact-SQL statement. It follows this basic syntax:

SYNTAX

```
CREATE LOGIN [login_name] FROM WINDOWS
```

Where: *login_name* is the name that the user or application will use to connect to SQL Server. If your login resides in a Windows domain, you must include the domain name followed by a backslash preceding the login name.

EXAMPLE 1 (Windows Login)

```
CREATE LOGIN [CORPHQ\amann] FROM WINDOWS
```

EXAMPLE 2 (Windows Group)

```
CREATE LOGIN [CORPHQ\SQLUsers] FROM WINDOWS
```

Example 1 grants the already existing Windows login named **amann** in the **CORPHQ** domain the right to access SQL Server. Example 2 is similar to Example 1, but grants the Windows group named **SQLUsers** in the **CORPHQ** domain the right to access SQL Server.

Granting Database Access

Before any user can access a database, or you assign a user or group to a database role, that user or group must have permission to access the database. As shown in Figure 16.1, once a user or group is allowed to gain access to SQL Server, it can access only the databases that it has been granted access. Granting database access is done with the **CREATE USER** Transact-SQL statement for either a SQL Server login or a Windows login and follows this syntax:

SYNTAX

```
CREATE USER [login_name]
```

Where *login_name* is the SQL Server or Windows login or group (depending on the authentication mode for your SQL Server). If your login resides in a Windows domain, you must include the domain name followed by a backslash preceding the login name.

EXAMPLE 1 (SQL Server Login)

```
CREATE USER [WebUser]
```

EXAMPLE 2 (Windows Login)

```
CREATE USER [CORPHQ\amann]
```

EXAMPLE 3 (Windows Group)

```
CREATE USER [CORPHQ\SQLUsers]
```

The **CREATE USER** Transact-SQL statement grants access to the specified user in the current database. Therefore, you must change to the desired database with the **USE** command or select the correct database from the dropdown list in Express Manager. Example 1 grants the SQL Server login named **WebUser** access to the current database. Example 2 grants the Windows login named **amann** in the **CORPHQ** domain access to the current database. Example 3 is similar to Example 2, but grants the Windows group named **SQLUsers** in the **CORPHQ** domain access to the current database. Of course, individual users must be assigned to the **SQLUsers** group for them to gain access to the current database.

Roles

Most Microsoft products implement role-based security, which is a set of permissions based on the job role performed by individuals that access the server. SQL Server security is implemented exactly the same way, except that there are three types of roles in SQL Server:

▶ **Server Roles** — Sets of permissions for users or groups that affect the entire server, which can cross databases.

▶ **Database Roles** — Sets of permissions for users or groups that affect a single database.

▶ **Application Roles** — Sets of user-defined permissions for users or groups that affect an application that accesses one or more databases on a server.

Before diving into the three types of roles in SQL Server 2005, it might be a good idea to refer back to Figure 16.1 to help you understand how roles work and how they are (or are not) affected by logins.

Server Roles

As the name implies, server roles affect the permissions set at the server level. Table 16.1 lists the server roles that are available in SQL Server 2005 Express. Because you cannot add, change, or delete these roles, they are referred to as *fixed* server roles.

Fixed Server Role	Description
bulkadmin	Can run the **BULK INSERT** Transact-SQL command.
dbcreator	Can manage a database itself in terms of creating, modifying, dropping, and restoring databases on a server.
diskadmin	Can manage disk files used for SQL Server storage.
processadmin	Can terminate SQL Server processes.
securityadmin	Can manage access to the server. Members of this role can manage server logins.
serveradmin	Can change server configuration settings and can also manage SQL Server services (shutdown, start, restart).
setupadmin	Can manage linked servers.
sysadmin	Can perform any task on a SQL Server, including all databases.

Table 16.1: SQL Server 2005 Express Fixed Server Roles.

Before a server role can be assigned to a user or group, that user or group must have a login to SQL Server with either a SQL Server or Windows login. This is shown in Figure 16.1. For more information about creating logins, see the section "Assigning Users to Roles" later in this chapter.

Database Roles

Database roles allow users or groups to receive permissions to perform certain actions within a database. Table 16.2 lists the database roles that are available in SQL Server 2005 Express. Unlike fixed server roles, new database roles can be added or deleted from SQL Server 2005. However, there are a set of default database roles that come out of the box, which are known as fixed database roles.

Fixed Database Role	Description
db_owner	Owns the database. Members of this role can perform any task within a database.
db_accessadmin	Can manage access to a database. Members of this role can manage logins and groups.
db_securityadmin	Can manage security permissions. Members of this role can manage membership in roles and groups, as well as manage permissions on database objects.
db_ddladmin	Can run DDL Transact-SQL commands to create data definition objects, such as tables, views, and stored procedures.
db_backupoperator	Can back up a database.
db_datareader	Can read data from tables in a database.
db_datawriter	Can write (insert, update, or delete) data to/from tables in a database.
db_denydatareader	Explicitly disallows members in this role from reading data in any table in a database.
db_denydatawriter	Explicitly disallows members in this role from writing data to any table in a database.

Table 16.2: SQL Server 2005 Express Fixed Database Roles.

Figure 16.1 shows that only users or groups that have a login into SQL Server and have been granted access to a particular database can be assigned to a database role. If you don't want to assign a user or group to a fixed database role, you can create your own and assign permissions to that new database role.

To create a new database role within a database, use the **CREATE ROLE** Transact-SQL Server command, according to this syntax:

```
CREATE ROLE role_name [AUTHORIZATION owner_name]
```

Where:

- ▶ *role_name* is the name of the database role that you wish to create

- ▶ *owner_name* is the name of the user or group that owns the new role

```
CREATE ROLE db_authors AUTHORIZATION db_securityadmin
```

In the above example, a new database role, called **db_authors**, is created in the current database and is owned by the **db_securityadmin** role. Making the new role being owned by the **db_securityadmin** role lets anyone who is already a member of this role manage the users assigned to this new role.

After the new database role is created and you assign permissions to the role, you assign users to that role as you would any other database role. See the sections "Assigning Users to Roles" and "Assigning Object Permissions" later in this chapter for more information about assigning roles.

Note:

You must be a member of the sysadmin fixed-server role or the **db_securityadmin** or **db_owner** database roles to use the **CREATE ROLE** command.

Application Roles

Application roles are typically used when an application enforces its own security mechanisms. By taking it as a given that security is already handled, you can bypass the process of assigning permissions to users and users to a role. Instead, you grant an application access to a database and give it a password that is used when the application creates a connection to the database. If you look at Figure 16.1, you'll see that the application role follows a different security path than does a server role or a database role.

That's because an application role does not need to have an explicit login into a server or even to a database the way a user or group does.

Caution:

You should know that using application roles requires that your application hard-code passwords into the application. This may be acceptable if your application needs basic privileges, but you should use this option with caution and understand that it may have security implications.

To add a new application role, use the **CREATE APPLICATION ROLE** Transact-SQL Server command, according to this syntax:

SYNTAX

```
CREATE APPLICATION ROLE role_name
WITH PASSWORD='password' [, DEFAULT_SCHEMA=schema_name]
```

Where:

▶ *role_name* is the name of the application role that you wish to create

▶ *password* is the password that your application will use to connect to SQL Server

▶ *schema_name* is the name of the default schema associated with the new application role. See Chapter 1 for a refresher on schemas.

EXAMPLE

```
CREATE APPLICATION ROLE app_PublicWeb WITH PASSWORD='WebPW@42$5'
```

In the above example, a new application role, called **app_PublicWeb** has a password of **WebPW@42$5**. Such a role can be useful for a public Web site that needs to connect to a SQL Server Express database, but doesn't have a separate SQL Server user account for each user.

Assigning Users to Roles

Whether you create your own database or application roles, or use the built-in fixed database or server roles, you must assign users or groups to that role. The next three sections outline how to assign users (logins) or groups to server, database, and application roles.

Fixed Server Roles

To add a login to a fixed server role, you use the **sp_addsrvrolemember** system stored procedure, which follows this general syntax:

```
SYNTAX
```

```
sp_addsrvrolemember 'login', 'role_name'
```

Where:

▶ *login* is the SQL Server or Windows login (depending on the authentication mode for your SQL Server). If your login resides in a Windows domain, you must include the domain name followed by a backslash preceding the login name.

▶ *role_name* is the name of the fixed server role that you wish to associate with the login. This role name must be one that is listed in Table 16.1.

```
EXAMPLE 1 (SQL Server Login:
```

```
sp_addsrvrolemember 'WebUser', 'securityadmin'
```

```
EXAMPLE 2 (Windows Login)
```

```
sp_addsrvrolemember 'CORPHQ\amann', 'diskadmin'
```

Example 1 assigns the **securityadmin** fixed server role to the SQL Server login named **WebUser**. Example 2 shows how to assign the **diskadmin** fixed server role to the Windows login named **amann** in the **CORPHQ** domain.

Database Roles

After you ensure the user or group has been granted access to a specific database, you can add it to the database role. To add a user or group to the database role, you use the **sp_addrolemember** system stored procedure, like this:

```
SYNTAX
```

```
sp_addrolemember 'role_name', 'security_account'
```

Where:

▶ *security_account* is the user or group that you wish to assign to the database role. If your login resides in a Windows domain, you must include the domain name followed by a backslash preceding the security account name.

▶ *role_name* is the name of the database role that you wish to associate with the login. This role name can be either a fixed database role or one that you create.

```
EXAMPLE 1 (SQL Server Login)
```

```
sp_addrolemember 'db_accessadmin', 'WebUser'
```

```
EXAMPLE 2 (Windows Login)
```

```
sp_addrolemember 'db_authors', 'CORPHQ\amann'
```

```
EXAMPLE 3 (Application Role)
```

```
sp_addrolemember 'db_authors', 'app_PublicWeb'
```

Example 1 assigns the **db_accessadmin** fixed database role to the SQL Server login named WebUser. Example 2 shows how to assign the **db_authors** user-defined database role to the Windows login named **amann** in the **CORPHQ** domain. Example 3 assigns the **db_authors** user-defined database role to the application role **app_PublicWeb**. For more information about application roles, see "Application Roles" in the next section of this chapter. If you look at Figure 16.1, you'll see that application roles can be assigned to database roles for the purpose of consolidating permissions, but they don't have to be. You can assign permissions directly to the application role if you wish.

Application Roles

As you learned earlier in this chapter, instead of creating and assigning individual logins for SQL Server and individual databases, you can create a single application role that will be used by an application (see Figure 16.1). Application roles can be created and assigned permissions to database objects, or to database roles for ease of administration. However, once you create the application role, you do not assign individual members to that role the way you do for server roles and database roles.

Assigning Object Permissions

Regardless of whether you created SQL Server logins, used Windows logins, or created application or database roles, the bottom-line is always the permissions that are assigned at the object level. Object-level permissions are assigned to specific objects that are created inside SQL Server, such as stored procedures, tables, views, and more.

Assigning object permissions to a user, group, database role, or application role is done with the **GRANT** Transact-SQL statement, which follows this basic syntax:

SYNTAX

```
GRANT permission [,...n] ON object TO principal [,...n]
```

Where:

- ▶ *permission* is the type of security permission that you wish to grant. Different types of objects allow different types of permissions. For example, you can grant **SELECT**, **INSERT**, **UPDATE**, and **DELETE** permissions on tables, but **EXECUTE** permissions on stored procedures. You can grant multiple permissions at the same time to the same groups with a single statement.

- ▶ *principal* is the login, user, group, database role, or application role name for which you will grant permissions.

EXAMPLE 1

```
GRANT SELECT, UPDATE ON Authors TO db_authors
```

EXAMPLE 2

```
GRANT EXECUTE ON usp_LookupData TO WebApp
```

EXAMPLE 3

```
GRANT EXECUTE ON usp_LookupData TO [CORPHQ\amann]
```

EXAMPLE 4

```
GRANT SELECT ON Products TO app_PublicWeb
```

The examples give you a good representation of the basics of how permissions work for not only SQL Server objects, but to users, groups, and roles. Example 1 grants **SELECT** and **UPDATE** permissions to the **Authors** table to the user-defined database role of **db_authors**. Example 2 grants **EXECUTE** permissions on a stored procedure named **usp_LookupData** to a SQL Server user named **WebApp**. Example 3 grants the same **EXECUTE** permissions on the stored procedure **usp_LookupData**, as does Example 2, but it assigns them to a Windows login **amann** in the **CORPHQ** domain. Notice in Example 3 that the Windows login name, including the domain name, is enclosed in quotation marks. If you don't do this, you'll receive a syntax error. Example 4 grants **SELECT** permissions on the **Products** table to the application role named **app_PublicWeb**.

Tech Tip:
There are many more options and permutations possible with the **GRANT** statement, so be sure to checkout Books Online if the examples provided in this chapter don't work for your scenario. However, these are the most common ways to use the **GRANT** statement.

Summary

Security is an extremely important topic. Although this chapter couldn't possibly cover every option or scenario that you might encounter, it does cover the basics of how SQL Server handles object security. When you install SQL Server 2005 Express, you choose the authentication mode—either SQL Server or Windows security. SQL Server lets you define logins that reside within the SQL Server system tables. Windows security uses the predefined login as created within your Windows domain.

Once you grant permission for a login to access SQL Server, you then grant access to one or more databases and assign permissions to individual SQL Server objects to those logins. Alternatively, you can create a database role that lets you group permissions to a logical role that a group of users might perform. Then you add members to that role. This is very similar to the way Windows groups collate users into one logical unit for administrative purposes. Alternatively, you can bypass the traditional login approach and create an application role that is used by an application. You then assign permissions to the application role or make the application role part of a database role.

Security should be considered carefully in your SQL Server 2005 Express databases. You should grant only the minimally required permissions to your users, groups, and roles to help keep your database secure. Additionally, you should refer to Chapter 6 to understand how network security is implemented in SQL Server 2005.

Did you know?

One of the biggest problems with connection issues to a SQL Server 2005 Express database is caused by the Windows Firewall, which is installed with Windows XP Service Pack 2. If it is configured correctly, you will not have any connectivity issues.

Chapter 17

Distributed Support

SQL Server 2005 includes limited support for multiple SQL Servers that are distributed in multiple locations. These servers can be located anywhere, as long as there is connectivity between the machines. In other words, multiple servers can be on your local area network (LAN), wide area network (WAN), or any other network topology.

There are two major types of distributed support in SQL Server 2005:

▶ **Replication** — Shares data with other servers, usually in large volumes. Replication existed in SQL Server prior to version 2005.

▶ **Service Broker** — Shares data with other servers, usually in smaller increments, known as messages. SQL Server Service Broker is new to SQL Server 2005.

There are additional ways to move data in and out of one SQL Server to another, such as distributed queries and linked servers, but neither of those technologies guarantees delivery of data in an automated fashion, so this chapter focuses on Replication and Service Broker.

Replication

Replication in SQL Server 2005 is based on a publisher/distributor model, where the following is true:

▶ A publication is comprised of one or more articles.

▶ A subscriber subscribes to a publication, which is called a *subscription*.

▶ A publisher publishes a publication.

▶ A distributor distributes a publication to a subscriber.

This publisher/distributor/subscriber model is known as the replication *topology*. This topology is shown in Figure 17.1.

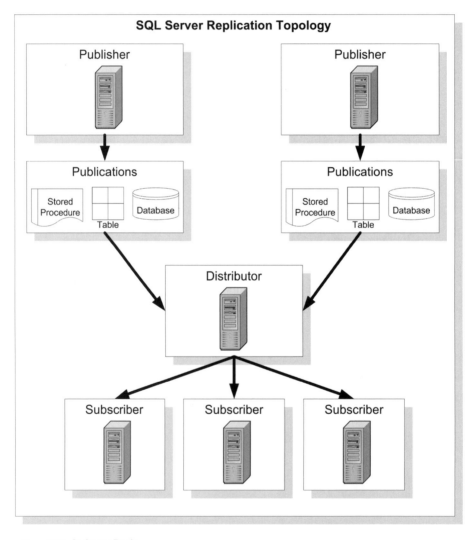

Figure 17.1: Replication Topology.

The support for replication in the Express edition of SQL Server 2005 is limited to the role of a subscriber. In other words, another SQL Server can publish data to a SQL Server 2005 Express instance. However, a SQL Server 2005 Express instance cannot publish to any other distributor.

Caution:

In the April CTP version of SQL Server 2005 Express, there was no graphical support for creating subscriptions in Express Manager. Instead, you have to use Transact-SQL to manage a SQL Server 2005 Express subscription.

The replication topology shown in Figure 17.1 works with three types of replication, which are all available in SQL Server 2005 Express (as long as it only serves as a subscriber):

▶ **Transactional** — Changes made to a publication by the publisher are replicated to a distributor and then on to a subscriber immediately. Transactional replication is appropriate for situations where data in remote systems needs to reflect changes in a "master" database, such as in the case of a centralized ordering system, where remote servers allow representatives to query current data.

▶ **Merge** — Similar to Transactional replication, but allows changes to be made in multiple places, either at the publisher or subscriber. SQL Server 2005 will merge the changes. Merge replication is appropriate for a situation where the data resides in multiple places for performance reasons, such as in remote offices that can each change customer data. At the end of the day, any changes will have to be synchronized amongst the servers.

▶ **Snapshot** — Sends data as it existed at a specific point in time, regardless of any updates being applied to the data. This is similar to a photo, where the snapshot is frozen at a specific point in time. Snapshot replication is appropriate for situations where you do not need up-to-the-minute access to your data. For example, a system that has to report daily sales would be appropriate for use with snapshot replication, because at the end of the day, a snapshot would be taken for all the data for the single day.

To add one more concept to the mix, in addition to the three types of replications supported in SQL Server 2005 Express, each subscription can be configured as:

► **Push** — The distributor is responsible for sending the data to the subscriber.

► **Pull** — The subscriber is responsible for requesting the data from the publisher.

Tech Tip:
You can also access the SQL Server 2005 Replication Management Object (RMO) programming model from any .NET language to configure and manage replication, but that is outside the scope of this book.

Implementing Replication with Transact-SQL

Remember that the Express edition of SQL Server 2005 can only subscribe to publications that exist on another edition of SQL Server 2005, such as SQL Server 2005 Standard edition. The process of creating a subscription is the following:

1. Create the subscription on the subscriber.

2. Update the subscription.

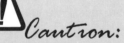

Caution:
Before you can create a subscription with SQL Server 2005 Express, you must have already configured the distributor and created the publication. In "non-Express" editions of SQL Server 2005, this is done by using the SQL Server Management Studio. See Books Online in these editions of SQL Server 2005 for more information on how to configure publications.

Creating the Subscription

To subscribe to a publication, you must first create the subscription. These stored procedures are used to create the subscription, depending on the type of subscription and replication you will be using:

▶ **sp_addpullsubscription** — Creates a pull subscription for transactional or snapshot replication.

▶ **sp_addmergepullsubscription** — Creates a pull subscription for merge replication.

▶ **sp_addsubscription** — Creates a push subscription for transactional or snapshot replication. Notice that there is no "push" word in the name of the stored procedure.

▶ **sp_addmergesubscription** — Creates a push subscription for merge replication.

The arguments for each type of subscription vary. Refer to Books Online to see the exact arguments for each stored procedure. As an example, here's the basic syntax to create a snapshot pull subscription:

SYNTAX

```
EXECUTE sp_addpullsubscription
    @publisher,
    @publication,
    @publisher_db
```

EXAMPLE

```
EXECUTE sp_addpullsubscription
    @publisher = 'PROD01',
    @publication = 'SalesPub',
    @publisher_db = 'Sales'
```

The example above creates a pull snapshot subscription to a publication named **SalesPub** in the **Sales** database on the **PROD01** server.

Updating the Subscription

An interesting dilemma for replication in SQL Server 2005 Express is that it does not include the SQL Server Agent service. Therefore, the updating, or synchronizing, of the subscription has to be done by other means. The Express edition of SQL Server 2005 relies on you configuring and using the little known application called Windows Synchronization Manager. This is available in Windows 2000 and later versions.

To use the Windows Synchronization Manager, follow these steps:

1. Click the **Start**⇨**Programs**⇨**Accessories**⇨**Synchronize** menu item to bring up the Windows Synchronization Manager. This is shown in Figure 17.2.

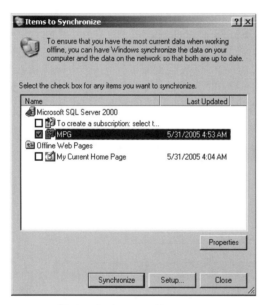

Figure 17.2: Windows Synchronization Manager.

2. To create a new subscription, click the top item and click the **Properties** button to configure a new subscription.

3. To manage an existing subscription, as indicated by the MPG item in Figure 17.2, click the desired item and then click the **Properties** button.

4. To synchronize a subscription between the distributor and the subscriber, click the **Synchronize** button.

For more information about using the Windows Synchronization Manager, visit the Microsoft Web site or Windows Help.

Service Broker

Typically, database designers and developers will design the database to create "work" tables that are used as a queue. These tables are used by one application to place data into the tables, while another application reads data from the tables at a later point in time. The application that reads the data might even flag a field in the table so that applications know that the data has been read. Alternatively, the application that reads the data might even delete data from the work table. The effect of this type of approach is to create an asynchronous application. This is the precise scenario that can benefit from Service Broker.

Service Broker lets you build asynchronous database applications, while shielding you from the incredible complexity of such applications. It is very difficult to write systems that guarantee reliable asynchronous transactions, so Service Broker handles this for you.

The process of implementing the SQL Server 2005 Express Service Broker application follows these basic steps:

1. **Create a message type** — Defines the characteristics of a Service Broker message. Messages are defined with the **CREATE MESSAGE TYPE** Transact-SQL statement.

2. **Create a contract** — Defines the characteristics of a dialog conversation. Contracts are defined with the **CREATE CONTRACT** Transact-SQL statement.

3. **Create a queue** — Defines the queue storage mechanism inside SQL Server 2005 for use by a Service Broker conversation. Queues are defined with the **CREATE QUEUE** Transact-SQL statement.

4. **Create a service** — Defines the routing and delivery characteristics of a Service Broker contract. Services are defined with the **CREATE SERVICE** Transact-SQL statement.

5. **Begin the conversation** — Marks the start of a conversation where messages will be placed on the queue. Conversations are started with the **BEGIN DIALOG CONVERSATION** Transact-SQL statement.

6. **Send a message to the queue** — Sends a message to the queue with an open conversation. This is defined with the **SEND** Transact-SQL statement.

7. **Receive the message from the queue** — Receives a message from a queue that has already been created. Messages are received with the **RECEIVE** Transact-SQL statement.

Listing 17.1 shows a sample of how easy it is to use the steps above to create the basic SQL Server 2005 objects used in sending and receiving basic Service Broker messages. In this listing, it uses a scenario where an application is in a manufacturing facility running on a wireless network, which is not necessarily reliable. This application is running on a remote computer that scans inventory products, by Stock Keeping Unit (SKU) as it is received into the warehouse. This scanned data must be sent to a central server, which collates the entire inventory.

```
-- Create two message types (one for request, one for response)
CREATE MESSAGE TYPE [InventoryScan_Request] VALIDATION = NONE
CREATE MESSAGE TYPE [InventoryScan_Response] VALIDATION = NONE


-- Create a contract for the inventory scan message types
CREATE CONTRACT [InventoryScan_Contract]
        (
        [InventoryScan_Request] SENT BY initiator,
        [InventoryScan_Response] SENT BY target
        )
-- Create a queue to store the Inventory Scan data
CREATE QUEUE [InventoryScan_Queue]
-- Create the service that uses the queue
CREATE SERVICE [InventoryScan_Service] ON QUEUE [InventoryScan_Queue]
        (
        [InventoryScan_Contract]
        )
```

Listing 17.1: Creating Service Broker Metadata Objects.

Once the objects are created that will control and store messages, the inventory data can be scanned as it is received and placed into the queue used by Service Broker. This is shown in Listing 17.2.

```
DECLARE @conversationHandle uniqueidentifier;
DECLARE @XMLMessage XML;
BEGIN TRANSACTION;

-- Begin the conversation with the InventoryScan_Service
BEGIN DIALOG CONVERSATION  @conversationHandle
    FROM SERVICE    [InventoryScan_Service]
    TO SERVICE      'InventoryScan_Service'
    ON CONTRACT     [InventoryScan_Contract]
    WITH LIFETIME = 600;        --10 minutes
-- Construct XML message from data received by scanner on UPC label
SET @XMLMessage = '
<InventoryScan_Request>
        <SKU>827188021111</SKU>
</InventoryScan_Request>
';       --This semicolon is necessary or SEND message will fail syntax

-- Send a message on the dialog
SEND ON CONVERSATION @conversationHandle
        MESSAGE TYPE [InventoryScan_Request]
        (@XMLMessage);
COMMIT TRANSACTION;
```

Listing 17.2: Sending a Message to the Queue.

Since the message is now contained within a queue, that is a database object, and it can be accessed just like it was a table with this line of code:

```
RECEIVE CAST(message_body as nvarchar(max)) as Message
FROM [InventoryScan_Queue];
```

This chapter doesn't cover Service Broker in too much detail because there is another book from Rational Press dedicated to this topic. *The Rational Guide to SQL Server 2005 Service Broker Beta Preview,* by Roger Wolter, shows you everything you need to know to build reliable asynchronous messaging applications using the new Service Broker feature of SQL Server 2005.

 Caution:

While the Express edition of SQL Server 2005 lets you implement Service Broker applications, there is one limitation. You cannot send and receive messages if there is no "paid" edition of SQL Server 2005 somewhere between the endpoints. In other words, if you have SQL Server 2005 Express send messages onto the queue, you must have either the Enterprise, Standard, or Workgroup editions receive messages from the queue (or vice-versa). If you have the Express edition send messages and another instance of Express edition receive messages, the messages cannot be viewed. No errors will occur; it just won't work.

Summary

SQL Server 2005 Express includes limited support for distributed systems. It includes replication support, but only as a subscriber. SQL Server 2005 Express cannot be a distributor or publisher of data to be replicated. However, other editions of SQL Server 2005 can be publishers and distributors. SQL Server 2005 also includes support for Service Broker to build asynchronous distributed applications. It includes full functionality in the Express edition of SQL Server 2005, but must have a paid edition somewhere along the line. This chapter showed you the basics of how to implement replication and Service Broker applications.

XML Support

All editions of SQL Server 2005 have greatly expanded support for XML over the SQL Server 2000 predecessor. In SQL Server 2000, if you wanted to store XML data, you'd have to do so in a text field, with virtually no support to process the XML structure as data. It was simply considered to be text. On the other hand, if you had data stored in relational tables, you could query the data and have the output formatted as an XML document that could be used by an application.

In SQL Server 2005, XML is supported directly in the database with a new **XML** data type. The general use of XML in SQL Server 2005 Express is covered in this chapter. There are more advanced topics related to XML that are not covered, such as XPath, XQuery, and schema binding. For more information on those topics, refer to Books Online.

When to Use XML

There is no "magic formula" to determine when to use XML. XML data might make sense under these scenarios:

- ▶ Data is sent to you that is already in XML format. A client may send an XML document that you wish to store exactly as it was sent. For example, a customer might send you an order in XML format.

- ▶ You need to store data where you do not know the number of columns. If you don't know the number of columns that will be necessary, you can't define a database schema for it. However, you can easily construct an XML representation of this data and store it in a single column in your database. Data of this type is referred to as *semi-structured* or *unstructured* data.

► The data is self-contained. This type of data does not reference any other table or conform to any rule. An example of self-contained data would be an unsolicited resume sent to SQL Server 2005 Express from a Web site. This resume would not be related to any specific job, employee, manager, or any other relational data that might be stored in SQL Server tables.

► You know the structure of the data and it could be stored in relational tables, but you need to construct an XML document to send to a vendor and you want to store an exact copy of that XML document as it existed at the time you sent it.

Once you determine whether you will store XML data in your database, you can use the techniques discussed in the rest of this chapter to store and retrieve XML data in your SQL Server 2005 Express databases.

XML Data Type

If you plan to store XML directly in the database you can define your table with the **XML** data type, which is new in all editions of SQL Server 2005. For example, you could create a table like the one shown in Listing 18.1.

```
CREATE TABLE BookData
      (
      ISBN            CHAR(10),
      Title           VARCHAR(100),
      PubDate         SMALLDATETIME,
      RetailPrice     SMALLMONEY,
      ONIX            XML
      )
```

Listing 18.1: Creating a Table with an XML Data Type.

In the example shown in Listing 18.1, there are four relational columns used to store book data:

► **ISBN** — Industry Standard Book Number. This number is currently a ten-digit number, but is changing to thirteen digits in 2007. This example keeps it simple at ten digits.

▶ **Title** — Stores the full title of the book.

▶ **PubDate** — Stores the publication date of the book.

▶ **RetailPrice** — Stores the retail price of the book, before any discounts.

▶ **ONIX** — XML structure used in the book publishing industry to send and receive book-related data with bookstores, wholesalers, and distributors.

Tech Tip:

If you would like to know more about the ONIX format, visit www.editeur.org/onix.html.

Writing XML Data

Assuming you have created the table shown in Listing 18.1, you can insert data into the table the same way as you would insert any other data, with the **INSERT** Transact-SQL statement, as shown in Listing 18.2.

```
-- Declare Temporary variable to hold XML data
DECLARE @tmpONIX XML

-- Assign XML data
SET @tmpONIX = N'
<Product>
        <RecordReference>1234567890</RecordReference>
        <NotificationType>03</NotificationType>
        <ProductIdentifier>
                <ProductIDType>02</ProductIDType>
                <IDValue>1932577165</IDValue>
        </ProductIdentifier>
        <ProductForm>BB</ProductForm>
        <Title>
                <TitleType>01</TitleType>
                <TitleText textcase = "02">The Rational Guide to SQL Server
⊃2005 Express Beta Preview</TitleText>
        </Title>
```

```
<Contributor>
        <SequenceNumber>1</SequenceNumber>
        <ContributorRole>A01</ContributorRole>
        <PersonNameInverted>Mann, Anthony T</PersonNameInverted>
</Contributor>
<NumberOfPages>224</NumberOfPages>
<BASICMainSubject>REF008000</BASICMainSubject>
<AudienceCode>01</AudienceCode>
<Publisher>
        <PublishingRole>01</PublishingRole>
        <PublisherName>Rational Press</PublisherName>
</Publisher>
<PublicationDate>2005</PublicationDate>
<SupplyDetail>
        <Price>
                <PriceTypeCode>01</PriceTypeCode>
                <PriceAmount>24.99</PriceAmount>
        </Price>
</SupplyDetail>
</Product>'

-- Insert data into table
INSERT INTO BookData
        (
        ISBN,
        Title,
        PubDate,
        RetailPrice,
        ONIX
        )
VALUES
    (
    1932577165,
    'The Rational Guide to SQL Server 2005 Express Beta Preview',
    '06/2005',
    24.99,
```

```
@tmpONIX
)
```

Listing 18.2: Inserting XML Data into a Table.

The main thing to notice in Listing 18.2 is the construction of the XML data and how it is stored in the table. In this example, an XML variable, named **@tmpONIX**, is populated with XML data, representing some of the data for this book as it would be represented in an ONIX XML file. This variable is then passed into the **INSERT** statement. The fact that it is XML structured data is irrelevant.

Reading XML Data

There are two ways to read XML data. The first is to read XML data that is stored in an **XML** data type. The second is to have SQL Server transform the results of relational data and return it as an XML document. Each is covered in the next two sections.

Reading an XML Data Type

To read data stored in an **XML** data type, it is as simple as executing a **SELECT** Transact-SQL statement. To retrieve the data stored in the database under Listing 18.2, you would simply execute this line of code:

```
SELECT * FROM BookData
```

Doing so in Express Manager results in a screen that looks like the one shown in Figure 18.1.

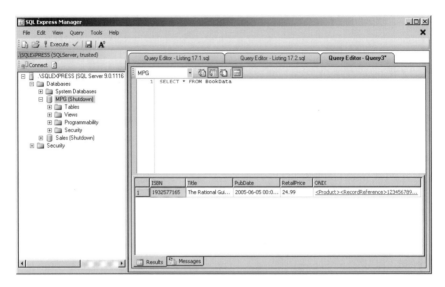

Figure 18.1: Executing a Query that Returns Data in an XML Data Type.

Notice in the results in Figure 18.1 that the **ONIX** field is shown as XML. To view the entire structure of the XML document, simply click the link. This brings up the screen shown in Figure 18.2.

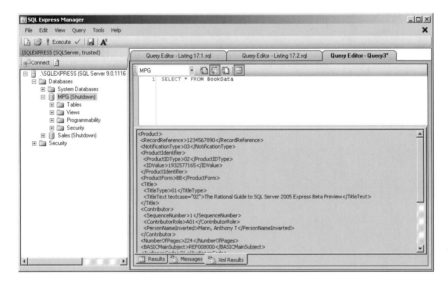

Figure 18.2: Viewing XML Documents in Express Manager.

Reading Relational Data as XML

Reading relational data and transforming it into an XML document is as simple adding a **FOR XML** clause to your **SELECT** Transact-SQL statements. At the end of your **SELECT** statement, you can indicate any of these XML modes:

▶ **FOR XML Auto** — Returns XML data based on the values in your **SELECT** statement.

▶ **FOR XML Raw** — Returns raw (non-nested) XML data.

▶ **FOR XML Explicit** — Returns the XML data by allowing you to specify the XML schema to which the returned document should be formed. This mode can be very difficult to implement.

▶ **FOR XML Path** — Similar to **FOR XML Explicit**, but easier to use.

If you specify the keyword **ELEMENTS** after the mode, the data will return column names as sub elements, instead of attributes. An example of how to use the **FOR XML AUTO** clause is shown in Listing 18.3.

```
SELECT *
FROM SalesHeader sh
    JOIN SalesDetail sd
        ON sd.OrderID = sh.OrderID
FOR XML AUTO, ELEMENTS
```

Listing 18.3: Example of Using FOR XML Auto, Specifying the ELEMENTS Keyword.

Listing 18.3 joins the **SalesDetail** to the **SalesHeader** tables on the **OrderID** field. This creates a hierarchy of data, where one order will have a single sales header, but possibly many detail fields, depending on the number of line items in an order. This statement returns XML data that looks like the one shown in Listing 18.4.

```
<sh>
  <CustomerID>5</CustomerID>
  <OrderID>10032</OrderID>
  <OrderType>3</OrderType>
  <CompanyName>Mann Publishing</CompanyName>
  <PONum>2334AR</PONum>
  <TotalSale>10322</TotalSale>
```

```
<Timestamp>2005-05-29T14:00:00</Timestamp>
<sd>
  <CustomerID>5</CustomerID>
  <OrderID>10032</OrderID>
  <LineNum>1</LineNum>
  <Quantity>2</Quantity>
  <Timestamp>2005-05-26T02:22:00</Timestamp>
</sd>
<sd>
  <CustomerID>5</CustomerID>
  <OrderID>10032</OrderID>
  <LineNum>2</LineNum>
  <Quantity>322</Quantity>
  <Timestamp>2005-05-29T13:58:00</Timestamp>
</sd>
</sh>
```

Listing 18.4: Results of Using the FOR XML AUTO Clause Using the ELEMENTS Keyword.

If you don't use the **ELEMENTS** keyword, your columns will be returned as attributes, like the results shown in Listing 18.5.

```
<sh CustomerID="5" OrderID="10032" OrderType="3" CompanyName="Mann
➲Publishing" PONum="2334AR" TotalSale="105.20">
  <sd CustomerID="5" OrderID="10032" LineNum="1" Quantity="2"/>
  <sd CustomerID="5" OrderID="10032" LineNum="2" Quantity="3"/>
</sh>
```

Listing 18.5: Results of Using the FOR XML AUTO Clause Without Using the ELEMENTS Keyword.

In Listings 18.4 and 18.5, the main element names in the hierarchy, sh and sd, were generated by the **SELECT** statement. The **SalesHeader** table is aliased as **sh** and the **SalesDetail** table is aliased as **sd**. Therefore, make sure to alias your table names as you wish to see them in the XML document. Also, each individual column being returned is shown as an element with its value being that which is stored in the table.

Summary

It used to be somewhat difficult to work with XML data prior to SQL Server version 2005. In all editions of SQL Server 2005 (including Express), working with XML data couldn't be easier. XML is considered to be a first-class database object, just like objects such as tables and stored procedures. Because of this deep integration, you can store XML data using the new **XML** data type, which is great for semi-structured and unstructured XML documents. You can also return data from relational tables as XML, although this support existed in SQL Server 2000 as well. This chapter showed you the basics of how to manage XML in a SQL Server 2005 Express database.

Did you know?

XML files are used extensively by many Microsoft products to store configuration data. For example, Visual Studio 2005 stores data set configuration information in an XML schema file with an xsd extension.

Extras

Glossary

Alias	Assigning a different logical name to a physical database object, such as a column in a table.
Application role	Set of permissions used by an application, not an individual user.
Authentication Mode	Mode where you indicate how SQL Server will authenticate logins; either Integrated (Windows) or SQL Server.
Class	Programming object that contains one or more functions or methods. Classes are defined when implementing CLR objects in a database.
CLR	Common Language Runtime set of libraries that are the basis for Microsoft's .NET strategy.
Clustered	Index where data is stored at the leaf level. Only one clustered index can be created on a table.
Common Language Runtime	See *CLR*.

Constraint	Database object that enforces business rules, such as a primary key constraint.
Data Access	Technology used to access SQL Server.
Database role	Set of permissions that are allowed to perform certain actions within a database.
Fillfactor	Percentage of free space that will be left free when SQL Server creates a new index page.
Fire	The action of a trigger being called.
Fixed server role	Set of permissions that are allowed to perform certain actions within a server. These roles are fixed and cannot be changed.
Foreign Key	Constraint that references fields in another table to enforce referential integrity.
Function	Code that executes and returns a value that can be used inline with Transact-SQL code.
Host	The ability to run CLR objects within another program, such as SQL Server 2005.
IDE	Integrated Development Environment, which is the graphical interface in Visual Studio 2005 that enables development for multiple facets of an application at the same time.

Index	Database mechanism based on B-Tree structure to quickly query data.
Instance	SQL Server installation that accepts connections. SQL Server 2005 Express uses a named instance called **SQLEXPRESS**.
Integrated Security	Logins are authenticated by either Windows or SQL Server.
Managed Code	Computer code written in a .NET language that is controlled, or managed, by the Common Language Runtime.
Method	Subroutine in a .NET assembly.
MSIL	Microsoft Intermediate Language, whereby the .NET Framework compiles code to the lowest possible level without needing to consider the type of CPU that will execute the code.
Named Pipes	Network library that communicates on a specific path called a pipe.
Non-clustered	Index stored in non-leaf pages pointing to data stored at the leaf-level of a B-Tree structure.
Object	Container for a specific type of data or code that will be executed in SQL Server. Object examples are tables, views, indexes, stored procedures, user-defined types, and more.
Pipe	See *Named Pipes*.
Primary Key	Constraint that enforces unique row values.

Replication	The automatic copying of data from one database to another, based on the publisher paradigm of publications, articles, and subscriptions.
Scalar	Refers to a single value that is used in a function, data type, or other SQL Server construct.
Schema	Database container for an object. The same object name can exist in multiple schemas.
Semi-structured data	Data that is partially structured in a logical way.
Service Broker	SQL Server 2005 technology that enables asynchronous messaging applications to be easily developed.
SNAC	SQL Native Client library that takes advantage of new SQL Server 2005 features for very rapid access to SQL Server 2005 servers.
SQL Native Client	See *SNAC*.
SQL Server Security	Method of verifying logins whereby user names and passwords are stored within SQL Server 2005 system tables.
Statistics	Statistical data based on a random sampling of index data and propagation.
Stored Procedure	SQL Server object that provides encapsulated functionality by executing one or more T-SQL or CLR assembly statements.

Surface Area	The relative exposure to security risks by SQL Server 2005. A large surface area exposes a server to higher risk than a small surface area. Therefore, it is recommended that features be turned off when not needed.
TCP/IP	Protocol for accessing a server based on IP address and port.
Transact-SQL	Implementation of the SQL-99 standard by Microsoft that includes additional support for SQL Server 2005-specific features.
Trigger	SQL Server object that executes when certain criteria are met. When the trigger executes, or fires, one or more T-SQL or CLR assembly statements are executed.
T-SQL	See *Transact-SQL*
UDT	See *User-defined Type*.
Unstructured data	Data that is completely void of any relational integrity.
User-defined Type	SQL Server object that can be created with either T-SQL or a CLR assembly to create data types, based on system data types to enforce consistency.
View	SQL Server object that is created based on one or more underlying tables. A view is often implemented as a security measure.
XCopy Deployment	Method of copying a Visual Studio 2005 project simply by copying it to a new folder.

XM   Express Manager graphical tool used to administer SQL Server 2005 Express databases.

XML   New data type available in SQL Server 2005 to handle semi-structured and unstructured XML data.

Notes

Notes

Notes

IMPORTANT NOTICE
REGISTER YOUR BOOK

Bonus Materials

Your book refers to valuable material that complements your learning experience. In order to download these materials you will need to register your book at http://www.rationalpress.com.

This bonus material is available after registration:

► Chapter: Advanced User Instances (RANU)

► Chapter: Advanced User-Defined Types

► Sample code used in the Book

Registering your book

To register your book follow these 7 easy steps:

1. Go to http://www.rationalpress.com.

2. Create an account and login.

3. Click the **My Books** link.

4. Click the **Register New Book** button.

5. Enter the registration number found on the back of the book (Figure A).

6. Confirm registration and view your new book on the virtual bookshelf.

7. Click the spine of the desired book to view the available downloads and resources for the selected book.

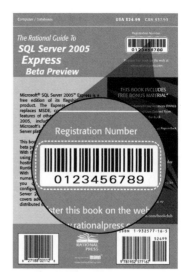

Figure A: Back of your book.